The Bible from Scratch

Available in the Bible from Scratch Series

The Bible from Scratch: The Old Testament for Beginners
Genesis from Scratch: The Old Testament for Beginners
Exodus from Scratch: The Old Testament for Beginners
The Bible from Scratch: The New Testament for Beginners
Matthew's Gospel from Scratch: The New Testament for Beginners
Mark's Gospel from Scratch: The New Testament for Beginners
Luke's Gospel from Scratch: The New Testament for Beginners

The Bible from Scratch

The Old Testament for Beginners

Donald L. Griggs

WJK Westminster John Knox Press
LOUISVILLE • KENTUCKY

First edition
Published by Westminster John Knox Press
Louisville, Kentucky

13 14 15 16 17 18 19 20— 20 19 18 17 16 15 14 13 12

Book design by Teri Vinson
Cover design by Dilu Nicholas

Library of Congress Cataloging-in-Publication Data

Griggs, Donald L.
The Bible from scratch : the Old Testament for beginners / Donald L. Griggs.— 1st ed.
p. cm.
Includes bibliographical references.
ISBN 0-664-22576-4 (alk. paper)
1. Bible. O.T.—Introductions. I. Title.

BS1140.3 .G74 2002
221.6'1—dc21

2001040751

♾ The paper used in this publication meets the minimum requirements of the American National Standard for Information Sciences—Permanence of Paper for Printed Library Materials, ANSI Z39.48-1992.

This adult Bible study is dedicated to

James A. Walther, Sr.

Bible scholar, author of *Kerygma: The Bible in Depth,*
and partner in teaching the Bible with youth and adults.

Writing, editing, teaching, and learning about the Bible is always more rewarding when you can share the journey with a friend.

Contents

Introduction

Do you have memories of your Sunday school teacher expecting you to memorize all of the books of the Bible in order? Can you recite them still?

Have you been in conversation with someone who quotes so many Bible verses that you feel intimidated and embarrassed about how little you know about the Bible?

Were you ever in a Bible study group when the leader instructed the class members to look up a Bible passage and you weren't quite sure where to look?

Have you been invited by someone to attend a Bible study group but thought of many reasons not to go because you were sure you would feel out of place?

If you have answered one or more of these questions in the affirmative, it may be that you have found the right resource to help you. After you have read this book, and perhaps been part of a group using the book for its study, you may not have memorized more Bible verses but you will find yourself becoming more comfortable with reading and studying the Bible. Researchers who asked adult members of congregations which topics they were "interested" or "very interested" in studying found that, of twenty-six possible topics, "the Bible" ranked the highest, with 77 percent indicating interest or high interest.[1] If your church is anything like the ones I know, it is obvious that 77 percent of the adult members are not involved in Bible study classes, groups, or programs. It is more likely closer to 15 to 25 percent.

I think the adults represented by the 50 to 60 percent not involved in Bible study in our churches are sincere in their desire to study the Bible but for a variety of reasons are not motivated to participate in such groups. Perhaps you can identify with those who would like to know more about the Bible, but are reluctant to seek out a Bible study group or accept an invitation to attend one. I have heard such reluctance stated as: "I'm sure everyone else in the group will know more about the Bible than I do." "Whenever people talk about the Bible I get confused and have a lot of questions that I'm afraid to ask because they seem like stupid questions." "I can't keep up with those who know where to find Bible

1. *Effective Christian Education: A National Study of Protestant Congregations,* funded by the Lilly Endowment and conducted by Search Institute, 1990.

passages." "To learn my new computer program I bought *Microsoft Office for Dummies*. That's what I need for learning the Bible." This book is written to address the concerns represented by such statements.

The Bible from Scratch: The Old Testament for Beginners is written to address other needs as well. You may be among those who have been attending Bible study groups for a number of years where the study has focused on specific passages or stories or books of the Bible. You have enjoyed such studies but have wished for an overview of the Bible so that you could see the relationships between its various parts. Or perhaps you have wished you could place the biblical events and characters in their historical context. If that is an interest of yours, this study guide will be a helpful resource. Another value of this book may be to provide you with a refresher course in which you review familiar material but look at it from a different perspective.

Whatever brings you to this book, I pray that God will bless you by the portions of the Bible that you read, by the thinking you do guided by the questions, and by the prayers you are prompted to pray. If you would like to join with others in the adventure of exploring the Bible, consider taking the initiative to form a group of fellow pilgrims on the journey. Ask your pastor or a Bible study leader in your church to guide such a group. When you are able to do Bible study with others in a group in your church, you are almost guaranteed to receive even more blessings than if you do the study solo.

If you find this study to be of value you may be interested in exploring the companion study, *The Bible from Scratch: The New Testament for Beginners*.

Part One

PARTICIPANT'S GUIDE

Chapter One
Introducing the Bible

Prayer Prompted by Scripture

Each chapter of this study begins with a prayer prompted by Scripture, with some suggestions for making it your own prayer.

The book of Psalms was the first prayer book of God's people. It is a collection of 150 prayers, songs, and expressions of faith by faithful believers who worshiped God before, during, and after their exile in Babylon in the sixth century BCE.[1] The collection was gathered over a period of several hundred years. Read the following portion of Psalm 92. In addition to reading these words as a prayer written centuries ago by a faithful believer, read the words as your personal prayer, as your expression of praise and thanksgiving.

> It is good to give thanks to the LORD,
>   to sing praises to your name, O Most High;
> to declare your steadfast love in the morning,

1. BCE is the abbreviation used today by biblical scholars to designate the time *B*efore the *C*ommon *E*ra. The older, and perhaps more familiar, abbreviation was B.C., designating the time *B*efore *C*hrist.

> and your faithfulness by night,
> to the music of the lute and the harp,
> to the melody of the lyre.
> For you, O LORD, have made me glad by your work;
> at the works of your hands I sing for joy.
> How great are your works, O LORD!
> Your thoughts are very deep!
>
> (Ps. 92:1–4)

Take a few minutes to meditate upon these words of the psalmist and to write a few key words, phrases, or short sentences to capture the meaning of Psalm 92 for you in response to the following questions.

For what do you give thanks and praise to God today?

What experiences are evidence for you of God's steadfast love?

What is a hymn that you like to sing to express your joy of God's great works?

What are some of God's great works for which you are especially joyful?

Approaching This Bible Study

If you are part of a Bible study group, you will receive the most benefit from this course if you read each chapter prior to the class session and participate actively in all of the suggested activities. Also:

- Be sure to bring your Bible and a pen or pencil.
- Be prepared to work individually or in small groups since this is not a lecture class.
- Don't be bashful about asking questions; there is no question that is silly or inappropriate.
- Don't be bashful about sharing your ideas, opinions, or interpretations, because often we will be assuming there is more than one appropriate answer to a question.

You might ask, "Which Bible should I use?" There are several possible answers.

- You could use whichever Bible you have available (see page 132 for a description of several Bible translations).
- If you have more than one Bible, it would be helpful to use at least two different translations for your study at home. Your understanding will be enhanced by additional translations.
- If you decide later that you would like to have a new Bible for this study, I would suggest that you consider purchasing a study Bible (see page 133–134 for suggestions). However, don't purchase a new study Bible immediately; wait for several weeks. After you have had some experience with Bible study, have seen examples of study Bibles, and have discussed with the class leader the features of various study Bibles, you will be ready to purchase one if you decide that is what you want.

Looking at the Whole Bible

Open your Bible, first to the table of contents and the pages immediately following. There are a total of sixty-six books in the Bible and some are very short and difficult to find. Therefore, in this study never feel embarrassed to turn to the table of contents to locate the book you are searching for. It is often quicker to use the table of contents even if you have memorized the order of all the books in the Bible.

In most Bibles, on one of the pages following the table of contents, you will find a page that lists all of the books alphabetically as well as in the order of their appearance. On that same page or another page you will also see the books of the Bible with their corresponding abbreviations. As you look carefully at these beginning pages, make a list of the major things you notice first and any questions that come to mind. For instance, you may have questions like, Why is this book called Holy Bible? Where does the word *Bible* come from? You will have an opportunity to share with the class your observations and questions when you meet next.

Things I notice	Questions I have
____________________	____________________
____________________	____________________
____________________	____________________
____________________	____________________
____________________	____________________

Look again at the table of contents. You probably notice titles of books with strange names, some of which may even be difficult to pronounce. If you wonder how to pronounce any of the book names, be sure to ask for assistance in class. As you have noticed, the Bible is divided into two major sections, the Old Testament (also called the Hebrew Scriptures) with thirty-nine different books and the New Testament with twenty-seven books. There is a variety of different types of literature or types of writings represented by those books. Some books are more historical while others are more like poetry; some contain a lot of laws and others are words of prophecy; some are letters and others are Gospels. Through the following chapters of this book and the sessions in the course, we will be exploring examples of these various types of writings.

Opening Your Bible to an Individual Book

Notice in the table of contents the page number for the beginning of the book of Genesis. Check to see whether or not your Bible has an introduction to the book of Genesis. Some Bibles, especially study Bibles, will have introductory articles to provide background information about the dating, authorship, setting, theme, and outline of each book of the Bible. Turn to the first page of Genesis and look with a curious eye at the whole page and all the little things that are there. First, make a list of the major things you notice and then any questions that come to mind, prompted by what you see on that page. If you are new to the Bible, don't hesitate to write down anything that comes to mind, even if it seems obvious to you. If you are a veteran of Bible reading, look with more care and curiosity and don't be afraid to write down anything that interests you.

Things I notice	Questions I have
________________	________________
________________	________________
________________	________________
________________	________________
________________	________________

Finding Books, Chapters, and Verses

Let's look at the matter of abbreviations and punctuation. Abbreviations sometimes differ from Bible to Bible. For instance, in the New Revised Standard Version (NRSV) you will see "Jon" for Jonah, in contrast to the New International

Examples of Bible Passages' Punctuation

Gen. 1:1 The name of the book appears, followed by chapter 1, followed by a colon, which separates the chapter number from the verse number. (Some Bibles use a period instead of a colon.) Notice that the number for verse 1 does not appear. The number for the first verse of every chapter is assumed.

Gen. 1:1–5 The dash means that we read chapter 1, verses 1 through 5.

Gen. 1:1–5, 9–13
The comma separates two distinct passages, which means that we read verses 1 through 5 and 9 through 13.

Gen. 1:1, 6, 9, 14, 20 and 26
This means that we read only the designated individual verses in chapter 1.

Gen. 1:1–2:4a This designation is less common. You will notice that verse 4 has two parts. Some translations have deterrmined that part *a* concludes the first narrative of creation and part *b* begins the second narrative. You will find this to be true in the NRSV but not necessarily in all other translations. However, there will be other occasions when you will want to separate parts of verses by identifying the parts as *a, b,* or *c.*

Version (NIV) where you will see "Jnh." Sometimes there will be different abbreviations in several editions of the same translation. On page 10 you will find a listing of the common abbreviations for the books of the Bible. It is helpful to become familiar with the particular abbreviations used in your Bible and to recognize that other Bibles may employ different letter symbols to identify the various books. Usually in Bible notes, footnotes, cross-references, and other citations of passages you will find abbreviations for names of the books rather than the complete spelling.

The matter of punctuation used in citing Bible verses and passages is also very important. Following are some common examples of abbreviations and punctuation.

The Scriptures

In several places in the New Testament there are references to "the scriptures." When we use the word *Scriptures* today we usually are referring to the whole Bible, the Old and New Testaments. However, at the time of Jesus and the beginning of the early church there was no New Testament. The good news of the gospel of Jesus Christ was being passed from one to another by the spoken word (oral tradition), and only later were those words put into writing and still later collected into what we have today as the New Testament. So the references in the New Testament to "the scriptures" were to the Hebrew Scriptures, the books of the Law, the Prophets, and the Writings. If you would like to get a head start on the next class session you may want to read the following passages (and you can practice the skill of searching for passages with abbreviations and punctuation): Lk. 4:16–21 and 24:13–35; Acts 8:26–38 and 17:1–5; Rom. 15:1–13, and 2 Tim. 3:10–17. As you read these passages, consider what specific Hebrew Scriptures (if any) are referred to, how those Scriptures are used, and what results from speaking, hearing, or reading those Scriptures.

Bible Skills and Tools Inventory

Take time before the next class to complete the Bible Skills and Tools Inventory found on page 9. All of the items refer to a skill or tool that is helpful for reading and studying the Bible. The results of this inventory when tabulated for the whole group will help your leader know what to emphasize and what to assume when planning future class sessions. There will be no judgment of your proficiency or lack thereof with these skills and tools. During the sessions of the course you will be introduced to various Bible study skills and tools. If your group is large, it may not be possible for each person to have separate Bible dictionaries, concordances, or other resources. If that is the case, your leader will provide photocopied pages from such books so that you will be able to use them in your exploring. For one-time use, for one class, this is not a violation of copyright laws. However, the most helpful tool of all for individuals to use in exploring the Bible is a study Bible.

Bible Skills and Tools Inventory

Each of the items below refers to a skill and/or tool that is helpful for studying the Bible. Check the statements in the column to the right that represent your own experience with the Bible.

1. Finding Bible passages by book, chapter, and verse is
   ___ no problem
   ___ sometimes difficult
   ___ a skill with which I need help

2. Identifying books of the Bible by their abbreviations is
   ___ no problem
   ___ sometimes difficult
   ___ a skill with which I need help

3. Checking the footnotes at the bottom of the pages of the Bible is a skill I use
   ___ often
   ___ occasionally
   ___ never

4. Using cross-reference notes to find sources or repetitions of passages in other places in the Bible is something I do
   ___ often
   ___ occasionally
   ___ never

5. Using a Bible dictionary is something I do
   ___ often
   ___ occasionally
   ___ never

7. Using a Bible commentary is something I do
   ___ often
   ___ occasionally
   ___ never

8. Using a Bible atlas is something I do
   ___ often
   ___ occasionally
   ___ never

9. Using different translations of the Bible is something I do
   ___ often
   ___ occasionally
   ___ never

10. The translations of the Bible I have are ______________________________.

11. The translation I prefer is ______________________________________.

12. Some things I hope this class will help me to learn or do with the Bible are
    ____
    ____.

Examples of Bible Books' Abbreviations

There should be a list of abbreviations that are used for the books of the Bible in the front of your Bible somewhere after the table of contents. Below are some commonly used abbreviations. A look at the list in your Bible will tell you which abbreviations your Bible uses.

Old Testament Books

Genesis	Ge	Gen
Exodus	Ex	Exod
Leviticus	Lv	Lev
Numbers	Nu	Num
Deuteronomy	Dt	Deut
Joshua	Js	Josh
Judges	Jg	Judg
Ruth	Ru	
1 Samuel	1 Sa	1 Sam
2 Samuel	2 Sa	2 Sam
1 Kings	1 Ki	1 Kgs
2 Kings	2 Ki	2 Kgs
1 Chronicles	1 Ch	1 Chron
2 Chronicles	2 Ch	2 Chron
Ezra	Ez	Eza
Nehemiah	Ne	Neh
Esther	Es	
Job	Jb	
Psalms	Ps	Psa
Proverbs	Pr	Prov
Ecclesiastes	Ec	Eccles
Song of Songs	SS	Song
Isaiah	Is	Isa
Jeremiah	Jr	Jer
Lamentations	La	Lam
Ezekiel	Eze	Ezek
Daniel	Da	Dan
Hosea	Ho	Hos
Joel	Jl	
Amos	Am	
Obadiah	Ob	Obd
Jonah	Jnh	Jon
Micah	Mi	Mic
Nahum	Na	Nh
Habakkuk	Hb	Hab
Zephaniah	Zep	Zeph
Haggai	Hg	Hag
Zechariah	Zec	Zech
Malachi	Ml	Mal

New Testament Books

Matthew	Mt	Matt
Mark	Mk	
Luke	Lk	
John	Jn	
Acts	Ac	
Romans	Ro	Rom
1 Corinthians	1 Co	1 Cor
2 Corinthians	2 Co	2 Cor
Galatians	Ga	Gal
Ephesians	Ep	Eph
Philippians	Php	Phil
Colossians	Col	
1 Thessalonians	1 Th	1 Thess
2 Thessalonians	2 Th	2 Thess
1 Timothy	1 Ti	1 Tim
2 Timothy	2 Ti	2 Tim
Titus	Tit	
Philemon	Phm	Philem
Hebrews	Hb	Heb
James	Ja	Jas
1 Peter	1 Pe	1 Pet
2 Peter	2 Pe	2 Pet
1 John	1 Jn	
2 John	2 Jn	
3 John	3 Jn	
Jude	Jd	
Revelation	Re	Rev

Chapter Two
The Books of the Law

The first five books of the Old Testament are known by several titles: "the Books of Moses," "the Law," "Torah," and "the Pentateuch." (*Pentateuch* is a Greek word meaning "five books.") These five books contain more than laws. They contain many narratives describing prehistory, the patriarchs, the deliverance of the Hebrews from slavery in Egypt, and their journey through the wilderness for forty years. The Hebrews understood *law* to be more than statutes, ordinances, rules, and laws. As *Torah,* a Hebrew word meaning "teaching" or "instruction," these books include the stories of God's mighty acts in creation and deliverance.

In this chapter we will focus primarily on the Hebrew concept of law and the general contents of the first five books. You will also be introduced to a helpful Bible study tool, a concordance.

Prayer Prompted by Scripture

We focus first on Psalm 119, which is a hymn of praise for the law of God. We start here because this psalm represents the fullest understanding of the meaning and the place of law in the life of the Hebrews. Read the following verses of Psalm 119 from the Contemporary English Version (CEV) as your prayer to God.

> I worship you with all my heart. Don't let me walk away from your commands. (v. 10)
> I praise you, LORD! Teach me your laws. (v. 12)
> Open my mind and let me discover the wonders of your Law. (v. 18)
> Help me to understand your Law; I promise to obey it with all my heart. (v. 34)
> You created me and put me together.
> Make me wise enough to learn what you have commanded. (v. 73)
> I won't ever forget your teachings, because you give me new life by following them. (v. 93)
> Your word is a lamp that gives light wherever I walk. (v. 105)
> If you will teach me your laws, I will praise you and sing about your promise,
> because all of your teachings are what they ought to be. (vv. 171–172)
> I am your servant, but I have wandered away like a lost sheep.
> Please come after me, because I have not forgotten your teachings. (v. 176)

Take a few minutes to meditate upon these words of the psalmist by responding to several questions. Write out a few key words, phrases, or short sentences to summarize the meaning for you of these few verses.

When you think of God's law, what comes to mind first?

When you think of the teachings of God in the Bible, what for you are the most important teachings to remember?

Which verse expresses best your prayer today? Why?

Exploring Psalm 119

Psalm 119 is the longest chapter in the Bible, with 176 verses. There are a number of other noteworthy features of this special psalm. In most Bibles, a larger space between one verse and another indicates the ending of one stanza and the beginning of the next. Turn to Psalm 119:1–8 and you will notice a larger space between verses 8 and 9, which indicates that verse 9 begins the second stanza. When you skim through the entire psalm you will notice that every stanza has eight verses and that there are twenty-two stanzas.

Psalm 119 is an acrostic psalm, which means that each of the eight verses of the first stanza begins with a word whose first letter is the first letter of the Hebrew alphabet—*aleph,* or the equivalent of the letter *a* in our alphabet. Each stanza continues in the same way in alphabetical order of the Hebrew alphabet, in which there are twenty-two consonants. Multiply eight verses per stanza by twenty-two letters (twenty-two stanzas) and the result is a psalm with 176 verses. I believe the writer of this psalm was someone of great faith in God who loved language and word puzzles as much as he loved the Law.

In addition to Psalm 119 being an acrostic, you will find in almost every verse a synonym or metaphor for the concept of law. The word *torah,* translated "law," appears at least once in each of twenty-two stanzas. Other words appear frequently: *decrees, statutes, ordinances, precepts, command(s), commandment(s), word(s),* and *promise.* In addition, you will find such words as *teaching(s), instruction(s), lamp, light, way(s),* and *judgments.* If you look at several different English translations you will find even more synonyms and metaphors for law in this psalm. Take a few minutes to read several stanzas of Psalm 119. Look at each verse to find the synonyms or metaphors that are present. In the margin, make a list of the ones you find.

The Five Books of the Law

In this brief introduction it is not possible to cover all of the important content of each of these first five books. The best we can do is to uncover some of the important information and key concepts. These first five books are often called the books of Moses. The authorship of Genesis, Exodus, Leviticus, Numbers, and Deuteronomy is attributed to Moses because he is seen as the great lawgiver. Certainly these books reflect the influence of Moses, who served faithfully as an intermediary between God and the Israelites. He was the one who was given the Ten Commandments by God. However, there is no internal evidence within the books themselves to suggest that Moses is actually the author. The five books are collections of narratives and laws that were first passed on orally and then centuries later assembled into written form. Let's consider some of the contents and characteristics of each of the five books.

Genesis

The word Genesis means "beginning." This book contains narratives about the beginnings of the human race (chaps. 1–11) and the people of God (chaps. 12–50). There are no laws, in the usual sense of the term, found in Genesis. The familiar stories of the beginning of the human race are: the creation and the garden of Eden (chaps. 1–3), Noah and the great flood (chaps. 6–9), and the tower of Babel (chap. 11). Chapters 12–50 contain the narratives of the families of Abraham and Sarah, Isaac and Rebekah, and Jacob and his four wives, who bore him twelve sons who were the origin of the twelve tribes of

Israel. We also find here the Joseph saga in chapters 37–50. The narratives in Genesis respond to a number of questions with which humankind has wrestled for centuries: Who is God? What is the origin of life? How do we know God? Who is the human being? What does God require of the human? What is the purpose of life? What is the origin of the people of Israel? What is the relationship between God and humankind? The responses to these questions do not provide logical, scientific answers but, rather, theological insights filled with wonder and mystery.

Exodus

The word *exodus* is from a Greek word meaning "going out," referring to the Hebrew slaves going out of Egypt into the wilderness on their way to the Promised Land. Chapter 1 serves as a transition between the Joseph narratives and those of Moses. The chapters that follow introduce Moses as a special servant of God with great powers and authority (chaps. 2–6), then present the many plagues against Pharaoh and the Egyptians (chaps. 7–12), the escape from Egypt and the first years in the wilderness (chaps. 13–18), the giving of the Ten Commandments (chaps. 19–20), additional laws (chaps. 21–35), and the building of the tabernacle (chaps. 36–40). The great themes of Exodus are deliverance, covenant, worship, faithfulness and obedience, unfaithfulness and disobedience, and God's sovereignty.

Leviticus

The English title of the book is based upon the Greek and Latin titles meaning "the book of the Levites." The Levites were priests of the tribe of Levi, one of the twelve sons of Jacob. The role of the priest was to preside over the sacrifices and other religious festivals. There were many rules for the priests to follow. The book of Exodus concludes with the building of the tabernacle, the portable sanctuary that accompanied the people in their forty-year journey from Egypt to the Promised Land. Some years after the people became settled in Canaan, the temple replaced the tabernacle as the central place for worshiping God. The book of Leviticus picks up where Exodus leaves off. It is a collection of rules and regulations governing many aspects of the cultic life of the people of Israel. The laws describe clearly what is clean, or holy, and what is unclean, or unholy; what is acceptable and what is unacceptable to God. The book is written as a series of commands from God directly to Moses and Aaron to deliver to the priests (in the early chapters) and to the people (in the later chapters). A key verse summarizes the thrust of the book: "You shall be holy to me; for I the LORD am holy, and I have separated you from the other peoples to be mine" (20:26).

Numbers

The English name for the book comes from the Greek through the Latin and relates to the two long census lists found in chapters 1 and 26 where the members of the twelve tribes of Israel are numbered. The Hebrew title for the book is "In the Wilderness," which describes the setting of the book and is derived from the first two words in the Hebrew text. Numbers continues where Exodus ends by telling the rest of the story of the Israelites' journey from Mount Sinai to Canaan, the Promised Land. There are a number of laws or instructions regarding how the people are to live, but most of the book consists of narratives regarding the struggles of their journey.

The book concludes with the people gathered at the banks of the River Jordan ready to cross the river and enter the land of Canaan. One of the best-known narratives is Numbers 13:1–14:44, which describes the spying mission to Canaan by twelve representatives, one from each tribe. We read of their adventure, their report, and the disagreement between the spies and Moses regarding whether or not to invade and occupy the land.

Deuteronomy

The title of this book is derived from the Greek for "the second law" or "a repetition of the law." Deuteronomy continues the story where it leaves off at the end of Numbers. The people are on the eastern bank of the River Jordan about to cross over into the Promised Land. Moses is prevented by God from accompanying them. The book is a series of speeches by Moses. Various interpreters have suggested there are between four and six speeches. For example:

- In speech 1 (chaps. 1–4), Moses reminds the people of God's mighty acts of deliverance from Egypt.
- In speech 2 (chaps. 5–26), Moses presents the Ten Commandments a second time and then interprets the meaning of the commandments. The people are reminded that they are to teach their children the meaning of the law.
- In speech 3 (chaps. 27–28), Moses reminds the people of the consequences of not obeying the law.
- In speech 4 (chaps. 29–30), Moses calls the people to be faithful, to keep the covenant they have made with God. A key verse is "Choose life so that you and your descendents may live" (30:19b).

- In chapters 31–32, Moses makes last preparations for the people to cross the Jordan. He appoints Joshua to be the leader of the people of Israel. He assembles all the elders of Israel, recites again the words of the law, and then sings a final song.
- Chapter 33 is Moses' last speech, a series of blessings for each of the tribes of Israel. (Chapter 34 concludes with the death of Moses on Mount Nebo.)

The book of Deuteronomy contains many laws, but there is nothing strikingly new; it is mostly a theological interpretation of the law.

Using a Bible Concordance

During the next class session you will learn how to use a Bible concordance. A concordance is a book that contains all or many of the key words of the Bible in alphabetical order with all or some of the verses that contain that word. The verses are presented in the order of the books of the Bible. There are three main types of concordances: (1) a very brief concordance that appears in the back of a study Bible, (2) a concise concordance that contains most of the key words of the Bible with representative key verses for those words, and (3) a comprehensive concordance that contains all of the key words of the Bible with all of the verses in which each word appears. Professors, teachers, and pastors use a comprehensive concordance for intensive biblical study. A concise concordance will serve well for most others who engage in Bible study. You will see on the next two pages examples of listings from each of the three types of concordances featuring the word *law*. Notice the number of verses in each example. The example of a comprehensive concordance includes only a portion of the verse references because to include them all would take more space than we have. However, you will see clearly the differences between the three types of concordances. These days many Bible students do not use a concordance in a book format. Instead, they have a version of the Bible installed on the hard disk of their computers and are able to find in seconds what might take minutes or hours to find using a book.

Conclusion

Reflect on what you have explored in this chapter. You have focused on the Hebrew understanding of law as presented in Psalm 119. You have reviewed some key features of each of the five books of the Law. And you have looked at the verse listings for *law* in three concordances. Spend a few minutes responding to several questions.

How important do you think the concept of law is in the Old Testament?

What impressed you most about Psalm 119 and the five books of the Pentateuch?

From what you know about the teachings of Jesus, how important was the law to him?

Three Different Concordances

In the two columns below, you will see examples of the differences between three types of concordances, featuring the word *law*. Notice that that word is represented by a boldface **l.** Verse citations from a concordance in a study Bible are very few and selective of key passages. In a concise concordance there are more verse citations, but they are still very limited and selective. In a complete concordance every verse with the word *law* is cited. If we were to add related words such as *laws, lawful,* and *lawless,* there would be many more citations.

Example as in a Study Bible

Exod.	24:12	I will give you the tablets of stone, with the **l**
Deut.	1:5	Moses undertook to expound this **l** as follows
	4:44	This is the **l** that Moses set before the Israelites
Josh.	1:8	This book of the **l** shall not depart out of your mouth
Ps.	1:2	their delight is in the **l** of the LORD
	119:97	Oh, how I love your **l**!
Jer.	31:33	I will put my **l** within them
Matt.	22:36	"Teacher, which commandment in the **l** is the greatest?"
Luke	24:44	everything written about me in the **l** of Moses
John	1:17	the **l** indeed was given through Moses.
Rom.	6:14	you are not under **l** but under grace.
	13:10	love is the fulfilling of the **l**.
Gal.	2:19	For through the **l** I died to the **l**.
	3:19	Why then the **l**?
Jas.	1:25	But those who look into the perfect **l**
	2:8	You do well if you really fulfill the royal **l** according to the scripture

Example as in a Concise Concordance

Exod.	12:49	there shall be one **l** for the native
Num.	5:29	This is the **l** in cases of jealousy
Deut.	4:44	This is the **l** that Moses set before the Israelites
	27:8	You shall write on the stones all the words of this **l**
	31:26	Take this book of the **l**
Josh.	8:34	And afterward he read all the words of the **l**
2 Kgs.	22:8	I have found the book of the **l** in the house of the LORD
Ezra	7:26	All who will not obey the **l**
Neh.	13:3	When the people heard the **l**
Ps.	1:2	their delight is in the **l** of the LORD
	19:7	The **l** of the LORD is perfect
	37:31	The **l** of their God is in their hearts
	119:44	I will keep your **l** continually
	119:97	Oh, how I love your **l**! It is my meditation all day long
Prov.	28:4	Those who forsake the **l** praise the wicked
	28:7	Those who keep the **l** are wise children
Jer.	26:4	walk in my **l** that I have set before you
	31:33	I will put my **l** within them
Matt.	5:17	I have come to abolish the **l** or the prophets
	12:5	have you not read in the **l** that on the Sabbath
Luke	2:39	finished everything required by the **l** of the Lord.
	5:17	Pharisees and teachers of the **l** were sitting near by
	10:26	What is written in the **l**? What do you read there?
	16:16	The **l** and the prophets were in effect until John came
John	1:17	The **l** indeed was given through Moses; grace and truth came through Jesus Christ
	8:5	in the **l** Moses commanded us to stone such women
Acts	6:13	This man never stops saying things against this holy place and the **l**
	13:15	After the reading of the **l** and the prophets
Rom.	2:13	For it is not the hearers of the **l** who are righteous in God's sight, but the doers of the **l** who will be justified
	3:31	Do we then overthrow the **l** by this faith? By no means!
	7:14	For we know that the **l** is spiritual
	8:3	For God has done what the **l** . . . could not do.
	13:10	love is the fulfilling of the **l**.
1 Cor.	9:21	To those outside the **l** I became as one outside the **l**
	15:56	The sting of death is sin, and the power of sin is the **l**.
Gal.	3:12	But the **l** does not rest on faith; on the contrary
	5:14	For the whole **l** is summed up in a single commandment
1 Tim.	1:8	Now we know that the **l** is good
Jas.	2:8	You do well if you really fulfill the royal **l** according to the scripture

Example as in a Complete Concordance

Exod.	12:49	there shall be one **l** for the native
	24:12	I will give you the tablets of stone, with the **l**
Lev.	11:46	This is the **l** pertaining to land animal and bird
	12:7	This is the **l** for her who bears a child, male or female
	24:22	You shall have one **l** for the alien and for the citizen
Num.	5:29	This is the **l** in cases of jealousy
	5:30	and the priest shall apply this entire **l** to her
	6:13	This is the **l** for the nazirites when the time
	6:21	This is the **l** for the nazirites who take a vow
	15:16	You and the alien . . . shall have the same **l** and the same ordinance
	15:29	you shall have the same **l** for anyone who acts in error
	19:2	This is a statute of the **l** that the LORD has commanded
	19:14	This is the **l** when someone dies in a tent
	31:21	This is the statute of the **l** that the LORD has commanded
Deut.	1:5	Moses undertook to expound this **l** as follows
	4:8	what other great nation has statutes and ordinances as just as this entire **l** that I am setting before you today?
	4:44	This is the **l** that Moses set before the Israelites
	17:11	You must carry out fully the **l** that they interpret for
	17:18	When he has taken the throne of his kingdom, he shall have a copy of this **l** written for him
	17:19	diligently observing all the words of this **l**
	27:3	You shall write on them all the words of this **l** when you have crossed over, to enter the land
	27:8	write on the stones all the words of this **l** very clearly.
	27:26	Cursed be anyone who does not uphold the words of this **l** by observing them.
	28:61	even though not recorded in the book of this **l**.
	29:21	the covenant written in this book of the **l**.
	29:29	to observe all the words of this **l**.
	30:10	decrees that are written in this book of the **l**.
	31:9	Then Moses wrote down this **l**, and gave it to the priests
	31:11	you shall read this **l** before all Israel in their hearing
	31:12	observe diligently all the words of this **l**
	31:24	When Moses had finished writing down in a book the words of this **l** to the very end
	31:26	Take this book of the **l** and put it beside the ark of the covenant of the LORD your God
	32:46	diligently observe all the words of this **l**
	33:4	Moses charged us with the **l**.
	33:10	They teach Jacob your ordinances, and Israel your **l**.
Josh.	1:7	being careful to act in accordance with all the **l**
	1:8	This book of the **l** shall not depart out of your mouth
	8:31	as it is written in the book of the **l** of Moses
	8:32	Joshua wrote on the stones a copy of the **l** of Moses
	8:34	And afterward he read all the words of the **l** . . . according to all that is written in the book of the **l**
	23:6	observe and do all that is written in the book of the **l**
	24:26	Joshua wrote these words in the book of the **l** of God
1 Kgs.	2:3	as it is written in the **l** of Moses
2 Kgs.	10:31	But Jehu was not careful to follow the **l** of the LORD.
	14:6	what is written in the book of the **l** of Moses.
	17:13	in accordance with all the **l** that I commanded your
	17:26	because they do not know the **l** of the god of the land
	17:27	teach them the **l** of the god of the land
	17:34	they do not follow the statutes or . . . the **l**
	17:37	The statutes and the ordinances and the **l**
	21:8	according to all the **l** that my servant Moses
	22:8	I have found the book of the **l** in the house of the LORD

Chapter Three
The Narratives of Genesis

In this chapter we will build upon what we learned in the previous chapter as we explore in more depth the storyline of Genesis. Because there are so many narratives in this first book of the Law, it is difficult to keep straight all the events and characters in these stories. In just a few pages we cannot master all of the material contained in the fifty chapters of Genesis. However, we can gain an overview of the book's major events and personalities.

Prayer Prompted by Scripture

Let's turn to another psalm, Psalm 78:1–8. This is one of five psalms identified as salvation history psalms.[1] These psalms were written to present a summary of the history of God's wondrous acts. When you add the contents of all five psalms together, you have an overview of the history of God's people from the creation to the establishment of the united kingdom under King David. Psalm 78 is the only

1. Other salvation history psalms are 105, 106, 135, and 136.

one of the five that provides a statement of purpose for reciting the history of God's dealings with the people of Israel. Read the first eight verses of the psalm:

> Give ear, O my people, to my teaching;
>   incline your ears to the words of my mouth.
> I will open my mouth in a parable;
>   I will utter dark sayings from of old,[2]
> things that we have heard and known,
>   that our ancestors have told us.
> We will not hide them from their children;
>   we will tell to the coming generation
> the glorious deeds of the LORD, and his might,
>   and the wonders he has done.
>
> He established a decree in Jacob,
>   and appointed a law in Israel,
> which he commanded our ancestors
>   to teach to their children;
> that the next generation might know them,
>   the children yet unborn,
> and rise up and tell them to their children,
>   so that they should set their hope in God,
> and not forget the works of God,
>   but keep his commandments;
> and that they should not be like their ancestors,
>   a stubborn and rebellious generation,
> a generation whose heart was not steadfast,
>   whose spirit was not faithful to God.

Take a few minutes to reflect on these words of the psalmist and on the questions that follow. Write out a few key words, phrases, or short sentences to summarize what these few verses mean for/to you.

Which of God's mighty acts and wondrous deeds would you like to share with your children or grandchildren or the children of your church?

When you read the psalmist's words, what are some reasons given for why we should be so diligent in telling the coming generations of God's wondrous deeds?

2. "Dark sayings from of old" seems somewhat foreboding. Another translation is "mysteries from the past" in Today's English Version (TEV). "Mysteries" may be more understandable to us than "dark sayings."

Think back to your childhood or adolescence or young adulthood. Who shared the good news of God's great deeds of salvation with you? Offer a prayer of thanksgiving for these important people in your life.

The Narratives of the Beginnings

Read about the beginnings of the universe and humankind in Genesis 1:1–2:4a and 2:4b–25. You will notice that in these two narratives are two different accounts of creation. There are many differences between the narratives and some similarities. The two narratives emerge from two different times and traditions, thus the differences. However, they both affirm that God is Creator and Lord of the whole creation from the beginning and forever. Chapters 3–4 tell of giving in to temptation by the first man and woman in the garden of Eden, Adam and Eve, and of their sons, Cain and Abel. Chapter 5 lists the ten generations from Adam and Eve to Noah. Chapters 6–9 present the narrative of Noah and his family and the great flood. Chapter 10 recounts the ancestors of the sons of Noah and where they settled after the flood. Chapter 11 presents the story of the tower of Babel and lists the family line from Shem, son of Noah, to Abraham.

The concepts and events in these first eleven chapters lead to many more questions than can be dealt with in this study. If you are interested in exploring more of the theological background related to these narratives, there are two resources that you will find very helpful. One is a good study Bible with notes and comments. A second is a Bible commentary on Genesis, of which there are several that are very appropriate for persons who are at the beginning stages of their Bible study adventure. Discuss with the leader of your group or your pastor what study Bible or commentary he or she would recommend and where you might be able to borrow or purchase such a resource.

Abraham and Sarah and Their Descendents

Genesis 12–23 presents the story of Abraham and Sarah

God calls Abram and Sarai to leave their homeland in Haran to go to a new land where God promises to make a great nation of them, to bless them, to make their names great, and where they will be a blessing to many. God makes a covenant with them and changes their names to Abraham and Sarah. God's promise to Abraham and Sarah is fulfilled, and Sarah in her old age bears a son, Isaac. Also in this section is the startling story of Abraham's obedience to God. He is instructed to offer Isaac as a sacrifice, and when he prepares to do it, God provides an alternative sacrifice in the form of a ram.

Genesis 24 is about Isaac and Rebekah

To find a wife for Isaac, Abraham sends a servant to his relatives in Mesopotamia, where he lived before migrating to Canaan. It was important for Isaac to have a wife from his father's family and not to marry a foreign woman in Canaan. This would fulfill God's promise to Abraham that he would be the father of many nations. The story of Isaac's servant seeking for him a wife and the subsequent meeting of Rebekah and Isaac is a beautiful story of God at work in their lives in order to fulfill the original promise God had made to Isaac's father.

Genesis 25–29 tells about Jacob and Esau, the sons of Rebekah and Isaac

Jacob, with his mother's help, tricks Esau out of his birthright and his father's blessing. Jacob flees from his home and has a dream while in the desert in which angels of God are ascending and descending a ladder between earth and heaven. Jacob hears God's promise that his offspring will be as numerous as the dust of the earth. Jacob builds an altar to worship God and promises to give one-tenth of everything to God (Gen. 28:10–22).

Genesis 29–31 tells of Jacob's life with Rachel and Leah and their father, Laban

Jacob is tricked into marrying Leah, the older of the sisters, when he really loves Rachel and desires for her to be his wife. There is much intrigue in these stories of Rachel, Leah, and their father, Laban. Leah gives birth to six sons. Rachel eventually becomes Jacob's wife and gives birth to two sons, Joseph and Benjamin, who become Jacob's favorites. Life with Laban's family in Haran is very difficult for Jacob, and after many years he is finally permitted to return to his home in Canaan.

Genesis 32–33 is the story of the reunion of Jacob and Esau

On his way home, Jacob is fearful of what he will experience when he meets Esau. In the middle of the night before meeting Esau, Jacob experiences a mysterious wrestling match with an unknown person. As a result of this experience he is blessed, his name is changed to Israel, and Jacob declares, "I have seen God face to face, and yet my life has been preserved." Esau journeys to Jacob to meet him. They are reunited and return to Canaan side by side.

Genesis 34–36 contains stories of violence, intrigue, faith, and death

Many years have passed between the events at the end of chapter 33 and the beginning of 34. A Canaanite rapes Jacob's daughter Dinah, and her brothers, Simeon and Levi, take violent revenge against the perpetrator and his people. This is the first act of violence between the Canaanites and the Israelites. The story is followed by Jacob's journey to Bethel, where he builds an altar to worship God. Then follows the birth of Benjamin and the deaths of Rachel and Isaac. This section closes with a lengthy list of the descendants of Esau.

Genesis 37–50 is the collection of the Joseph stories

Genesis 37:2a introduces the saga of Joseph with the words, "This is the story of the family of Jacob." Thus begins the longest section of the book of Genesis. Joseph is sold into slavery by his jealous brothers and is taken to Egypt. In Egypt, after many years, Joseph becomes a governor in charge of the grain storehouses. At the time of a famine in Canaan, when his family has gone to Egypt to secure supplies of grain, Joseph's identity is revealed and he and his brothers are reunited. The famine has become so severe in Canaan that all of Joseph's family move to Egypt, where they settle and continue to live for many years. Finally, there is the moving account of the death of Jacob, Joseph mourning his father's death, and Joseph again forgiving his brothers for the evil they did against him. The book ends with the death of Joseph.

Whether the narratives of Genesis are familiar or unfamiliar, you should not be surprised that they are often amazing and confusing. When you read this part of the Bible, remember that the words were written several millennia ago in a place and time and from a worldview very different from our own. The narratives are not so much historical accounts as they are theological statements to account for the origins of the world, of humanity, and of the nation of Israel. They are theological affirmations about the meaning of covenant between God and human beings, about the providence of God, about the faithfulness and sinfulness of the people, and about relationships between members of families and clans. A key question to keep before you as you read these prehistory narratives is, What do these stories tell me about the nature of God and the nature of human beings and their relationship to each other?

Practicing with Footnotes

Most Bibles include footnotes throughout the chapters of the sixty-six books. Skim through the pages of Genesis and you will notice a variety of footnotes of several kinds and purposes. Look at several examples from the NRSV:

- Gen. 1:1: "In the beginning when God created[a] the heaven and the earth . . ." Look at the bottom of the page and you will see footnote *a:* "Or *when God began to create* or *In the beginning God created.*" This means that there are at least two additional ways to translate the original Hebrew words.
- Gen. 1:2b: ". . . while a wind from God[b] swept over the face of the waters." The footnote suggests two other possible translations. Notice that the Hebrew word for *wind* could also be translated as *spirit.*
- Gen. 17:5: "No longer shall your name be Abram,[b] but your name shall be Abraham.[c]" This changing of the name from Abram to Abraham is an important passage, and the footnotes reveal to us the meaning of the two names in Hebrew. *Abram* means "exalted ancestor" and *Abraham* means "ancestor of a multitude."
- Gen. 29:17: "Leah's eyes were lovely.[f]" The footnote tells us that the meaning of the Hebrew word rendered "lovely" is uncertain.
- Gen. 41:43b: "Bow the knee.[g]" The footnote suggests that the original is apparently an Egyptian word.

You will find other kinds of footnotes. Some will state, "Other ancient authorities suggest . . ." Unfortunately, there are no original Hebrew manuscripts. The oldest manuscripts found by archaeologists were written or copied many centuries after the originals. There are a variety of such manuscripts and, as might be expected, there are minor variations between them. In some editions of the Bible, the ancient authorities or manuscripts are identified by an abbreviation. If your Bible includes such abbreviations, you will find their explanation on one of the beginning pages. Take a few minutes to skim several chapters of Genesis or another book of the Bible to see what kinds of footnotes you find. As you read your Bible and notice a footnote after a word, you will know how to discover more about the meaning of that word or phrase.

A Search and Find Exercise

In order to review some of what we have been exploring in this chapter related to the narratives in Genesis, fill in the following blanks. If you don't remember the correct answers, you will find them by using the designated Bible references.

Abraham and __________ his wife (18:9)
had a son, __________ (21:3) who married __________ (24:67)
and they had twin sons, ________ and _______ (25:24–26).
Jacob and his wives had twelve sons, who became the patriarchs of the twelve tribes

1. ________________ (35:22–26)
2. ________________
3. ________________
4. ________________
5. ________________
6. ________________
7. ________________
8. ________________
9. ________________
10. ________________
11. ________________
12. ________________

There are several name changes in Genesis. The changes are significant.

From Abram to _____________, which means _________________ (17:5)
From Sarai to _____________, which means _________________ (17:15)
From Jacob to _____________, which means _________________ (32:28)

Other names have significant meanings in the original Hebrew:

Isaac means ______________________ (21:6)
Esau means ______________________ (25:25)
Jacob means ______________________ (25:26)
Benjamin means ______________________ (35:18)

A Search and Find Exercise *(continued)*

There are several important places where persons encountered God in some way. Read the passages related to each place and write a brief statement describing the significance of the place.

Haran (12:4)

Moriah (22:2)

Bethel (28:19)

Peniel (32:30)

From the narratives of Genesis what do you learn about the following?

God

Human beings

Sin

Covenant

God's will for humanity

Chapter Four
From Egypt to Canaan

Beginning with the events in Exodus and concluding with the death of Joshua in the book by that name, we have a period of history spanning about one hundred years. There are many wonderful stories in the books of Exodus, Numbers, and Joshua that tell of the deliverance of the people of Israel from slavery in Egypt, their forty-year journey in the Sinai wilderness, and their moving into Canaan, the Promised Land. This chapter covers a lot of stories for which we can only skim the surface. We will be looking at the landscape of this portion of the Old Testament as if we are flying over it at 35,000 feet in a jet plane. Fasten your seatbelts as we take off for a quick flight over a dynamic landscape of conflict and courage, fear and faith, defeat and victory, doubt and trust.

Prayer Prompted by Scripture

All who have served God through the centuries have had experiences of doubt and trust. There are times when each of us has doubts about God's will for the world and our own lives, or perhaps even doubts about God's nature or existence. The writers of Psalms were persons of profound faith in God who felt themselves in intimate relationship with God. Yet more than half of the 150 psalms are examples of faithful people complaining and expressing doubts to God. These are called psalms of lament; they include both community laments and personal laments. For some people, it is difficult to read the book of Psalms from beginning to end because they are turned off by the many laments. However, one of the characteristics of psalms of lament is an element of praise of and/or trust in God. (In addition to an element of trust being present in the psalms of lament, there are also a number of other psalms identified as psalms of trust. The most familiar of these is Psalm 23.)

Our prayer for this chapter of our journey through the Old Testament is guided by expressions of trust found in selected verses from several psalms. Read these words slowly and prayerfully.

> I keep the LORD always before me;
> because he is at my right hand, I shall not be moved.
> Therefore my heart is glad, and my soul rejoices;
> my body also rests secure. (Ps. 16:8–9)
> The LORD is my light and my salvation;
> whom shall I fear?
> The LORD is the stronghold of my life;
> of whom shall I be afraid? (Ps. 27:1)
> God is our refuge and strength,
> a very present help in trouble.
> Therefore we will not fear, though the earth should change,
> though the mountains shake in the heart of the sea;
> though its waters roar and foam,
> though the mountains tremble with its tumult. (Ps. 46:1–3)
> For God alone my soul waits in silence;
> from him comes my salvation.
> He alone is my rock and my salvation,
> my fortress; I shall never be shaken. (Ps. 62:1–2)
> Remember your word to your servant,
> in which you have made me hope.
> This is my comfort in my distress,
> that your promise gives me life.
> . . . .
> Your statutes have been my songs
> wherever I make my home.
> . . . .
> This blessing has fallen to me,
> for I have kept your precepts. (Ps. 119:49–50, 54, 56)

Read the words of the psalmist again. This time, select one line or verse that speaks to you in a special way at this very moment. Focus on that line or verse. Repeat the words several times. Close your eyes and repeat the words over and over, slowly and prayerfully. Take this prayer of trust in God with you today and tomorrow. You could repeat this process with other psalm verses day after day.

Moses, a Man of Doubt and Trust

The main character of the collection of stories in Exodus and Numbers is Moses. He was a Hebrew child born in Egypt. As a young man he was observed killing an Egyptian overseer who was mistreating a Hebrew slave. He escaped to Midian, where he married, settled down with a family, and served as a shepherd of his father-in-law's flocks. One day while tending the flocks, Moses experienced God calling him from the midst of a bush that was burning but wasn't consumed. God called Moses to return to Egypt to become the instrument of God to deliver the people of Israel from the burden of their slavery. Moses was reluctant to accept God's call of service and responded with many excuses. Read Exodus 3:1–4:20.

An important part of this narrative is God's response to Moses' request to know God's name (Exod. 3:13). The name revealed to Moses is "I AM WHO I AM" (notice the footnote in the Bible text). In the original Hebrew, the word (transliterated in English) is YHWH, the holy name for God. This name for God is so holy that to this day, Jews do not speak the name but instead say "Adonai," which in English is rendered as "LORD." Notice that the letters are in small capitals. Look again at the psalm verses above and you will see the divine name printed in this way. Look at psalms in your Bible to find other examples. Now look again at Exodus 3:14 and you will see the holy name for God is also in small capital letters.

Twenty Examples of God's Mighty Acts of Deliverance

It is a detailed, dynamic storyline between the birth of Moses and the death of Joshua. The major events of the story can be found in the following movements:

- Exodus 1 sets the stage for the larger story.
- Exodus 2–20 covers Moses' birth to the giving of the Ten Commandments at Mount Sinai.
- Numbers 10:11–35:34 and Deuteronomy 34 cover the story from leaving Mount Sinai to the death of Moses, before entering Canaan.
- Joshua 1:1–24:33 presents the story of entering and settling in Canaan up to the time of Joshua's death.

This is a long, dramatic, and complicated story, but it is worth reading if you have the interest and the time. What follows is an abbreviated version of the story featuring key passages that emphasize important persons, places, and events in twenty episodes, with some very brief comments.

1. Moses' birth and early years (Exod. 2:1–25)

Moses' parents are from the tribe of Levi, which became a tribe of priests. Pharaoh fears the rise of the Israelites because of their many births so he commands that all male babies be killed. God protects Moses with the help of his mother and sister and the daughter of Pharaoh. Moses is raised in Pharaoh's court but with sympathies for the Hebrews. As a young man he observes an Egyptian overseer abusing a Hebrew slave, so Moses comes to his defense and kills the Egyptian. Fearing for his own life, he escapes to the land of Midian.

2. Moses called by God to return to Egypt (Exod. 3:1–4:31)

Moses is called by God to return to Egypt. He offers five excuses and each one is countered by God: (1) Moses says, "Who am I that I should go to Pharaoh?" and God responds, "I will be with you." (2) Moses says he doesn't know the name for God. God reveals the name: I AM WHO I AM. (3) Moses says, "But suppose they do not believe me or listen to me." God provides a staff that holds miraculous powers. (4) Moses complains that he is not eloquent and is slow of speech. God promises to be with his mouth and to teach him what he is to speak. (5) Moses says, "O my Lord, please send someone else." God is angry with Moses but grants that his brother Aaron will be his spokesman.

3. Moses and Aaron's first efforts to free the Hebrew slaves (Exod. 5:1–6:12)

Moses and Aaron's first attempt to seek the release of the Hebrew slaves is not only unsuccessful, but Pharaoh makes the plight of the slaves even more difficult by not providing straw for the making of bricks while still demanding the same production.

4. The nine plagues on the Egyptians (Exod. 7:12–11:10)

These four chapters describe a series of nine plagues: blood in the river, frogs, lice, flies, diseased livestock, boils, hail, locusts, and darkness. The sequence is similar in each: (1) Moses and Aaron appeal to Pharaoh with the familiar words, "Let my people go," (2) a plague occurs by the power of God working through Moses and Aaron, and (3) Pharaoh's heart is hardened. After several of the plagues, Pharaoh begs for relief and promises to let the people go, but then his heart is hardened even more. The Hebrews are never affected by the plagues.

5. The passover (Exod. 12:1–29)

In a final, devastating plague, the angel of death strikes and kills the firstborn of all the Egyptian families and animals. But because the blood of a sacrificial lamb is smeared on the doorposts of the homes of the people of Israel, the angel of death passes over their homes. This final plague eventuates in the escape of the Israelites from Egypt, the saving act of God that is remembered to this day in the Festival of Passover.

6. The exodus. (Exod. 12:29–42 and 13:17–14:4)

The people of Israel escape from their bondage with their families and their flocks and herds. They are led by God toward the Red Sea and the wilderness instead of taking a shorter route through the land of the Philistines. In this passage is the first mention of a pillar of cloud by day and a pillar of fire by night. The cloud and the fire are symbols of God's presence going before them, leading the way through the wilderness. One incidental fact is that Moses takes the bones of Joseph with him on the journey (13:19).

7. The crossing of the sea (Exod. 14:5–31 and 15:19–21)

Once again, Pharaoh, following his usual behavior, reneges on his promise and decides to pursue the Israelites to capture them and return them to his control. The Israelites complain to Moses that it would have been better to be slaves than to die in the wilderness or drown in the sea. By the power of God at work through him, Moses raises his arm with the staff of God, and the waters part to allow the Israelites to pass through. When he lowers his staff the waters return, drowning the pursuing army of Pharaoh. After crossing through the waters there is great celebration with the songs of Moses and Miriam, his sister. These texts are among the oldest in the Hebrew Scriptures. When you look at the map on page 37 you will notice that the traditional route of escape does not actually cross the Red Sea but more likely a marshy area further to the north. The name in Hebrew, *yam suph,* translated "Red Sea," may also be translated "Sea of Reeds."

8. Manna and quail (Exod. 16:1–35)

The Israelites complain to Moses and Aaron because they are hungry and there is no food for them. They say again that it would have been better to die in Egypt at the hands of Pharaoh than to die of hunger in the wilderness. In response to their complaining, and their need, God provides manna and quail, bread and meat, to sustain them.

9. At Mount Sinai (Exod. 19:1–20:21)

There are many mountains in the southern Sinai Peninsula, so the exact location of Mount Sinai is unknown. The people of Israel are camped at the base of the mountain. Moses is the intermediary, the priest, between God and the people. We gain a sense of the holiness of God symbolized by the smoke, fire, thunder, and trumpet blasts. No one is even to touch the mountain or they will die. The people are to consecrate themselves for three days before they are to receive God's commandments. Only Moses is permitted to approach God on the mountain. There God gives the Ten Commandments to Moses to give to the people so that they may live faithfully in relation to God and with one another. The first four commandments have to do with reverence toward God and the other six relate to relationships among people.

10. The ark of the Lord and the tabernacle (Exod. 25:1–26:37)

These two chapters and those that follow give detailed instructions regarding the building of the ark of the Lord and the tabernacle. These are not built until after the second set of tablets is given to Moses for the people. The ark was to be the receptacle for carrying the tablets on which the commandments were inscribed. The tabernacle would be a portable, tent-like sanctuary that the Israelites could carry with them on the journey. The ark was placed in the holy of holies within the tabernacle. The tabernacle, also called the tent of meeting, served as the sacred place where God would dwell in the midst of the people. Once the people became settled in Canaan, the temple in Jerusalem replaced the tabernacle.

11. The golden calf (Exod. 32:1–3:3)

Moses has been on the mountain with God for a long time. The people are restless and demand of Aaron that he make gods for them. Aaron gives in to the people and crafts a golden calf for them to worship. When Moses returns and sees what they have done, he is so furious he throws the tablets to the ground, where they break. Then he burns the golden calf with fire. The story continues with violence and disobedience and ends with God's promise to send an angel before them as they journey, but God will not be among them as before.

12. Second set of Ten Commandments (Exod. 33:12–34:35)

We read in 34:6–7 of God's gracious, merciful, loving nature. Moses seeks to restore himself and the people to the good grace of God. In this narrative we see again the holiness of God and the special relationship between God and Moses. Moses is given a second set of tablets with the Ten Commandments, which he presents to the people to guide their living.

13. Complaints in the wilderness (Num. 11:1–34)

We move from Exodus to Numbers, where the story of the wilderness journey continues. There continues to be a refrain of complaints. The Israelites remember the good things they had to eat in Egypt and seem to forget the misery of their life as slaves, so they complain to Moses. Moses has had it with the people and complains to God, "Why have I not found favor in your sight that you lay the burden of all this people on me? . . . I am not able to carry this people alone, for they are too heavy for me" (vv. 11, 14).

14. Spies sent to explore Canaan (Num. 13:1–3, 16–33)

Twelve men, one from each tribe, are sent to spy out the land of Canaan. They return with a report of fortified towns and a very strong people, and bring with them samples of the bountiful fruit of the land. Caleb and Joshua encourage the people to proceed to occupy the land, but the other ten persuade everyone to refrain from going forward.

15. The people rebel against God and Moses (Num. 14:1–45)

Again the people rebel and talk about choosing a captain to lead them back to Egypt. Moses, Aaron, Caleb, and Joshua plead with the people to trust God to lead them, but they will have none of it and threaten to stone them. God responds, "None of the people . . . who have tested me ten times and have not obeyed my voice, shall see the land that I swore to give to their ancestors" (vv. 22–23). So the sojourn in the wilderness will take many more years.

16. Renewal of the covenant (Deut. 29:1–18 and 30:11–20)

The Israelites journey forty years in the wilderness. They arrived in Moab, to the east of the Jordan River. A covenant with God had been established at Sinai years earlier. Now, as one of his final acts as their leader, Moses engages the people in an act of renewing their covenant with God.

17. Joshua to succeed Moses, and the death of Moses (Deut. 31:1–29 and 34:1–12)

Moses served God faithfully all the years of the journey from Egypt to Canaan. He was on Mount Nebo and able to see the Promised Land across the river. But

Moses was prevented from crossing over with the people because of an earlier incident. In Num. 20:1–13, the people had complained once again about having no water to drink and had wished they had never left Egypt. Moses used his staff and struck a rock twice and water gushed forth. Bible scholars do not agree on an explanation of this punishment of Moses by God. Whatever the reason, Moses dies on Mount Nebo, and the people mourn his death for thirty days. The text records, "Never since has there arisen a prophet in Israel like Moses, whom the LORD knew face to face" (34:10). Leadership of the people passes to Joshua, who had been blessed by Moses for the task.

18. The crossing of the Jordan (Josh. 1:1–18 and 3:1–4:24)

Joshua is commissioned by the Lord to lead the people, and the people promise to follow him as they had Moses. The crossing of the Jordan is like a religious procession, with the ark of the Lord being carried by the priests leading the way. The priests stop in the middle of the river and the water ceases to flow, allowing the people to cross over on dry ground, reminiscent of their crossing of the sea forty years earlier.

19. The fall of Jericho (Josh. 5:13–6:27)

The crossing of the Jordan occurs near the town of Jericho. Jericho was a walled, heavily fortified town and had to be conquered in order for the Israelites to occupy the land. This highly symbolic story tells of seven priests carrying seven trumpets in front of the ark of the Lord for seven days. On the seventh day they march around the walls seven times. On the seventh time, the people are commanded to shout and the priests to blow their trumpets. The walls of the city collapse. The number seven is special: the creation had happened in seven days; it is a sign of perfection and completeness.

20. The people renew their covenant with God (Josh. 24:1–28)

The chapters of the book of Joshua between the fall of Jericho and chapter 24 are filled with battles, as Joshua leads the people to settle in the land of Canaan. The boundaries are set for the twelve tribes. In chapter 23, Joshua, in his old age, calls the people together to deliver his farewell address. In chapter 24, Joshua reminds the people of God's saving acts and calls them to recommit themselves to serve the Lord by obeying the commandments they had received.

Thus, we conclude a long story of God's saving acts on behalf of the people of Israel, the people of the covenant. Yet this long story is just the beginning of the story of God's special relationship with the people of the covenant. We have been introduced to two great leaders, Moses and Joshua. We have seen how fickle the people are in their commitment to obey God and to follow Moses. We have seen how loving, forgiving, and faithful God is toward the people of Israel. There is much we can learn about God and about what is expected of those who are called to be in special relationship with God.

Take some time to reflect on these narratives describing the journey of the Israelites from Egypt to Canaan.

What impresses you most about the story?

What are the biggest questions you have about the story?

Which parts of the story would you like to explore in more depth?

What did you learn about God and God's people through these narratives?

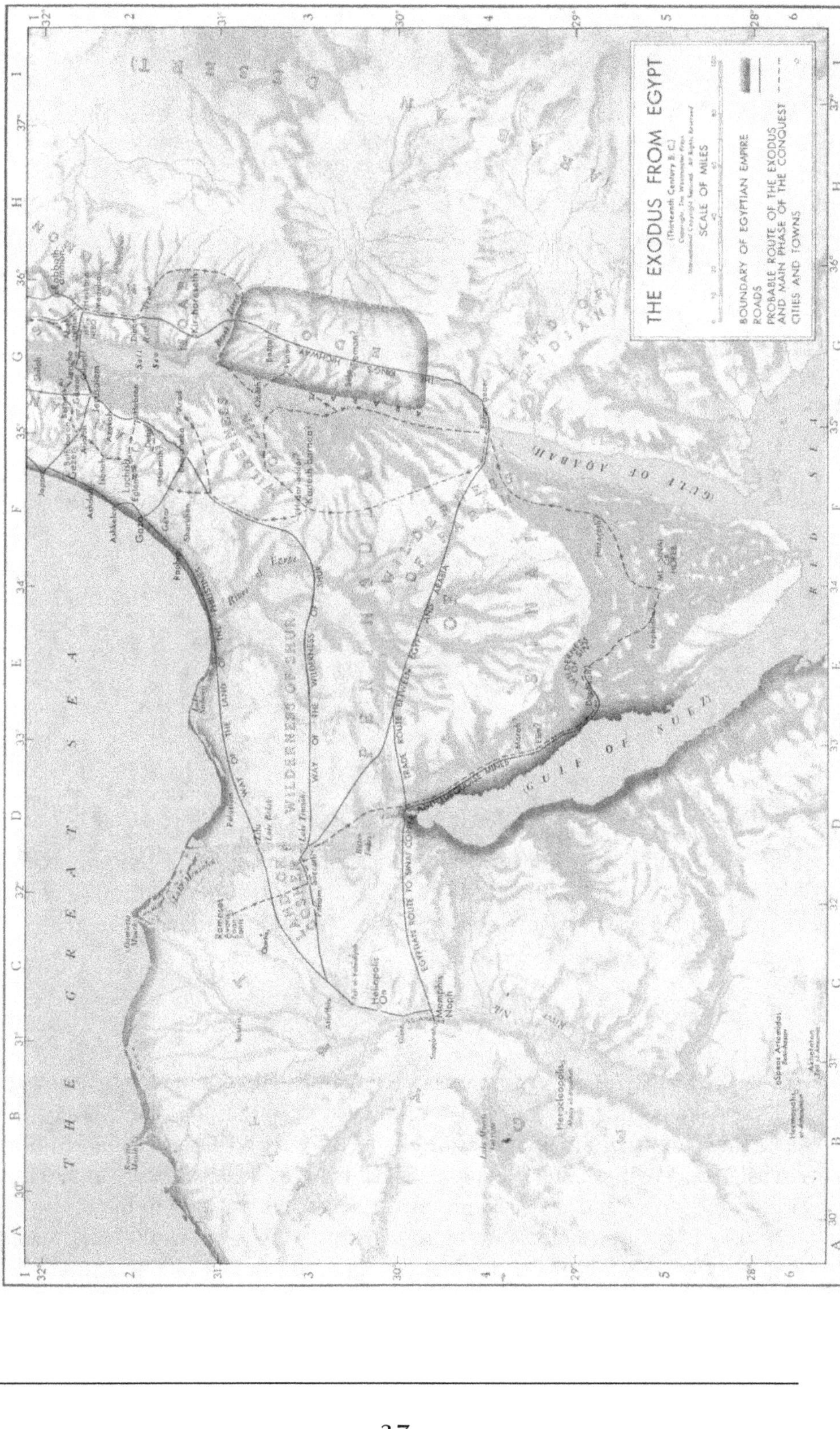
THE EXODUS FROM EGYPT
SCALE OF MILES
BOUNDARY OF EGYPTIAN EMPIRE
ROADS
PROBABLE ROUTE OF THE EXODUS AND MAIN PHASE OF THE CONQUEST
CITIES AND TOWNS
THE GREAT SEA
GULF OF SUEZ
GULF OF AQABAH
WILDERNESS OF SHUR
WAY OF THE LAND OF THE PHILISTINES
WAY OF THE WILDERNESS OF SHUR
Heliopolis
On
Memphis
Noph
Heracleopolis

Chapter Five
From Joshua to Nehemiah

Our exploration in this chapter will cover a long span of biblical history, approximately eight hundred years. In this study, Joshua is the "bridge person." We concluded with his death in the last chapter and begin our sweep of history with him in this chapter. Our goal is to gain a little information about some of the key characters and events in this eight-hundred-year period of history.

Prayer Prompted by Scripture

You have already discovered there are many translations and paraphrases of the Bible. A translation is ordinarily a product of a group of Bible scholars who base their translations upon the original Hebrew and Greek versions. Some translations are more literal, which means that they seek to preserve the meaning of the words and the structure of the sentences as close to the original as possible. Other translations are more dynamic, which means that they seek to express the meaning of the original text in a vocabulary and structure that is more like the way we use the English language today. Both types employ the latest findings in biblical scholarship and attempt to provide reliable and authentic translations. A paraphrase of the Bible is usually the result of one person working to convey the language of the Bible in the more popular, contemporary vernacular of the day. Often a paraphrase will reflect some of the particular biases and emphases of the one preparing the paraphrase. What follows is a paraphrase of Psalm 16 from *The Message: The Psalms in Contemporary Language* by Eugene H. Peterson. May this be your prayer to God as well as the psalmist's prayer.

> Keep me safe, O God,
> I've run for dear life to you.
> I say to God, "Be my Lord!"
> Without you, nothing makes sense.
> And these God-chosen lives all around—
> what splendid friends they make!
> Don't just go shopping for a god.
> Gods are not for sale.
> I swear I'll never treat god-names
> like brand-names.
> My choice is you, GOD, first and only.
> And now I find I'm *your* choice!
> You set me up with a house and yard.
> And then you make me your heir!
> The wise counsel GOD gives when I'm awake
> is confirmed by my sleeping heart.
> Day and night I'll stick with GOD;
> I've got a good thing going and I'm not letting go.
> I'm happy from the inside out,
> and from the outside in, I'm firmly formed.
> You canceled my ticket to hell—
> that's not my destination!
> Now you've got my feet on the life path,
> all radiant from the shining of your face.
> Ever since you took my hand,
> I'm on the right way.

Now that you have read/prayed this paraphrase of Psalm 16, read/pray the same psalm in one or two other translations with which you are more familiar. Notice how Eugene Peterson transforms the more formal language into images and metaphors that correspond with our everyday experience. As you compare Psalm 16 in *The Message* with other, more formal translations, reflect on whether or not you think Peterson has captured the meaning of the text. Does it speak to you in a new and refreshing way?

Where Are We in the Bible and in History?

Before proceeding, we need to get our bearings, since we will be dealing with a very long period in the history of the people of Israel. Turn to the table of contents in your Bible. You will see that the book of Joshua follows the fifth book of the Pentateuch, Deuteronomy. From the book of Joshua to Nehemiah there are eleven books. We will visit briefly eight of these books that are often called books of history. Originally there were three different collections in the Hebrew Scriptures: The Law, The Prophets, and The Writings. These collections were gathered and then accepted as Scripture over many centuries, in that order. The books we will be looking at (except for Ezra and Nehemiah) are included in the collection of The Prophets, or, more accurately, the Former Prophets. The books of Ezra and Nehemiah are included in the collection of Writings, as is Ruth, which we will consider later.

Two books we will not be considering are 1 and 2 Chronicles, also included in the collection of Writings. These two books cover the same period of history as 2 Samuel through 2 Kings, though from a different context and with a more positive spin on the history of the people and leaders of Israel. The books of Samuel and Kings present the people and their leaders with all their faults as well as their strengths.

In addition to looking at the table of contents of your Bible, turn to page 49 to review the timeline you will find there. It is very difficult to ascertain with certainty the exact dates when particular events happened and particular persons lived, so treat most of the dates as approximate. (This is symbolized by the letter *c,* for *circa,* meaning "approximately.")

Key Persons and Events from Joshua to Nehemiah

Joshua
(Josh. 1:1–9; 14:1–15, and 24:14–28)

Joshua was one of twelve spies who were sent to Canaan to check out the opposition they would face and to return with some of the fruits of the land. He and Caleb were the only two of the twelve who thought the Israelites could prevail against the Canaanites. He was a faithful assistant to Moses and was commissioned by God and Moses to lead the people into the Promised Land. Joshua served God faithfully and called the people to renew their covenant with God prior to crossing the Jordan and putting themselves in danger as they sought to occupy the land. Joshua led them in battle and then apportioned the land to the twelve tribes. Joshua was the "bridge person" between the journey in the wilderness and the settling of the land of Canaan.

Gideon
(Judg. 6:1–24 and 7:1–22)

We focus on Gideon as the representative judge of the Israelites. He was the fifth in a series of thirteen judges. The judges were more like military leaders than what we think of as arbiters of justice. The period of the judges lasted for more than two hundred years. The narratives of each of the judges follow a similar pattern:

1. "The Israelites did what was evil in the sight of the LORD" (6:1).
2. Because of their sin, "the LORD gave them into the hand of [their enemy]" (6:2).
3. "The Israelites cried to the LORD on account of [their enemy]" (6:7).
4. "The LORD sent a prophet to the Israelites" (6:8).
5. The judge defeated the enemy and brought a period of peace to the people of Israel: "So the land had rest for forty years" (8:28).
6. After the death of the leader, the people reverted to their old ways: "As soon as Gideon died, the Israelites relapsed and prostituted themselves with the Baals [the gods of the Canaanites]" (8:33).

The two selected passages above, featuring Gideon, tell us of his call by God to be the deliverer of the people and of his success in warfare. At the time of his call, Gideon, like Moses, had excuses for why he should not be the one to do what God wanted done. And, as with Moses, God countered Gideon's excuse by giving him the power to do what God wanted done.

Hannah
(1 Sam. 1:1–28 and 2:18–26)

We are introduced to Hannah, the wife of Elkanah, in the first book of Samuel. Unable to have children, she prayed earnestly to the Lord for a son and promised that if she were to be so blessed she would dedicate him to the Lord's service. Eli, the priest, observed Hannah and thought she was intoxicated because she appeared to be mumbling to herself. She told him she was praying and revealed to him the nature of her prayer. God answered her prayer, and in due time Hannah gave birth to a son and named him Samuel, which means "God heard." Hannah kept her promise. After she had weaned Samuel, she took him to Shiloh and presented him to the priest, Eli. (Shiloh was where the ark of the Lord was kept during the period of the judges.) When Hannah and her husband, Elkanah, went to the sanctuary at Shiloh annually to offer their sacrifice, they would be blessed by Eli. In addition to making their sacrifice, Hannah would bring a new robe for Samuel each year.

Samuel (boy)
(1 Sam. 2:11–26 and 3:1–4:1–2)

Eli raised Samuel in the service of the Lord at Shiloh. Eli had other sons who were scoundrels; they had no regard for the LORD or for the duties of the priests to the people. "Samuel's call by God is a beautiful story showing God's persistence and a human's misunderstanding about God's call. Three times God called, "Samuel, Samuel." And three times Samuel responded by going to Eli and saying, "Here I am," thinking it was he who called. Eli realized that it was God who was calling Samuel and told him that the next time he heard his name called he was to respond, "Speak, for your servant is listening." The Lord revealed to Samuel that the sons of Eli would be killed and he would grow up in Shiloh knowing that the Lord was with him. The people knew that Samuel was one who was blessed by the Lord and was to be trusted.

Samuel (man)
(1 Sam. 7:15–8:22 and 10:17–27)

As Joshua was a "bridge person" between the wilderness journey and settling in Canaan, so Samuel was a "bridge person" between the period of the judges and the reign of the kings of Israel. Samuel is identified as a priest (2:35), a prophet (3:20), and a judge (7:15). When Samuel became old, he made his sons to be judges over the tribes of Israel, but they were not faithful to the Lord. The people prevailed upon Samuel to appoint a king to reign over them like the kings who ruled other nations. At first Samuel refused their request, believing that only the Lord God should rule as their king. God revealed to Samuel that he should listen to the people, so he obeyed. He called the people together and chose by lot a son of the family of Kish who was of the family of the Matrites who were of the tribe of Benjamin. The one chosen was Saul, who stood head and shoulders above all the rest. Then in the presence of the people, Samuel admonished them regarding the duties of the king. Samuel was very reluctant to name a king, and he lived long enough to see that Saul was a failure and was eventually rejected, even by God. Samuel grieved over Saul's misdeeds and disobedience to God. He also presided over the naming and anointing of David to be the second king of Israel.

Saul
(1 Sam. 10:1–27; 14:47–15:35)

Saul was a tall, handsome man who fought many successful battles against the enemies of the Israelites. However, Saul was never able to conquer his primary enemy, the Philistines. Despite his power as king and his prowess as a military leader, Saul was a very insecure man. Samuel and the Lord rejected Saul because of his unfaithfulness, though he served as king for many years. During much of his reign, Saul sought to kill David, who became very popular with the people because of his successes in battle against the Philistines, symbolized by his slaying of Goliath. Even his daughter Michal and son Jonathan conspired against Saul to protect David. Saul died in battle from a self-inflicted wound because he did not want to be killed by his enemy.

David (boy)
(1 Sam. 16:1–23; 17:12–27, 38–51)

The story of David as a boy is a familiar one. He was the youngest son of Jesse and was a shepherd of his father's flocks. Samuel was directed by God to the household of Jesse to anoint the next king of Israel. All of Jesse's older sons were presented to Samuel, but none was pleasing to the Lord. Finally, David was summoned from the fields where he was tending the flocks. And the Lord told Samuel, "Rise and anoint him; for this is the one." Though David was anointed by Samuel to become the next king, it would be many years before he would actually reign as the king of Israel.

David's encounter with Goliath is one of the most familiar stories in all of the Old Testament. All of Saul's army were frightened by the mighty giant of the Philistine army. David appeared on the scene with food for his brothers. With God's power present with him and the courage of one who had protected his sheep from wild animals, David faced Goliath and killed him with one stone from his sling. David continued to find favor in the Lord's sight.

David (in hiding)
(1 Sam. 18:6–16; 19:11–18; 22:1–5; and 23:1–14)

David enjoyed much success in leading his small band of warriors against the enemies of Israel. He became so popular that the people sang songs about him as the mighty warrior. The song, "Saul has killed his thousands, and David his ten thousands," was very displeasing to Saul. He became jealous of David and sought to kill him. David was protected against all of Saul's intrigue and threats by God's presence with him, by the loyalty of Michal, his wife, and Jonathan, his dearest friend (Saul's daughter and son) and by his own cunning. There were times when David could have killed Saul, but he chose not to. David continued for many years to lead a band of soldiers who waged battle after battle, successfully defeating the enemies of Israel. It was only after the death of Saul that David came out of hiding to become the second king of Israel.

Jonathan
(1 Sam. 20:1–42)

Jonathan was the oldest son of Saul and would rightly have been in line to succeed him as king. He was a courageous warrior, and in one incident his action of overcoming a Philistine outpost was the act that turned the tide of the battle. His father was jealous of his success and sought to kill Jonathan, but the soldiers protected him from Saul's wrath. Jonathan recognized in David a peer in valor and devotion to the Lord and befriended David, so they became even closer than brothers. On several occasions Jonathan was an advocate for David with Saul. When Saul attempted to capture David, it was Jonathan who provided the warning and the protection David needed to escape. Saul learned of Jonathan's loyalty to David and threw a spear at his son in an attempt to kill him. David and Jonathan remained loyal friends to the end. Jonathan died at his father's side, in the same battle where Saul killed himself.

David (king)
(2 Sam. 5:1–5; 6:1–23; and 11:1–27)

After the death of Saul, it was time for David to emerge from hiding to become the second king of Israel. At Hebron, the elders of Israel anointed David as king when he was thirty years old, and he served as king for forty years. During those years, David continued to be victorious in battle and to serve the Lord. He established his stronghold in Jerusalem and arranged for the ark of the Lord to be brought there. David continued to be loyal to Jonathan. He welcomed Jonathan's crippled son Mephibosheth into his home to eat at his table. Another story—not so admirable—tells of David's adulterous affair with Bathsheba, the wife of Uriah, a soldier in David's army. When David learned that Bathsheba was pregnant, he arranged for Uriah to be killed in battle so he could take Bathsheba as his wife. The prophet Nathan confronted David with his sin, and he was very remorseful for what he had done and begged for God's forgiveness. David is remembered as a shepherd of flocks and of the nation of Israel, as a courageous and successful warrior, as a faithful servant of God, and as one who sinned and was forgiven. In addition, many of the psalms are attributed to David as the author.

Nathan
(2 Sam. 7:1–17; 12:1–25 and 1 Kgs. 1:38–40)

Nathan was a prophet of God during the reigns of David and Solomon. Nathan's name means "gift of God." We read of his involvement on three important occasions. First, David consulted with him regarding building a house, or temple, for God. God spoke to Nathan, saying that the tabernacle, or tent, had served well throughout the journey in the wilderness and during the struggles to occupy Canaan and that it would continue to serve as the house for God's presence. David was not to build a temple, but his son Solomon would. God promised that David's house would be expanded in the form of a dynasty. The second time we encounter Nathan is when he confronts King David and brings God's judgment upon him for his sinful relationship with Bathsheba. The third important occasion where Nathan appears is many years later at the end of David's life when he and Bathsheba conspire to convince David to name Solomon as his successor.

Solomon
(1 Kgs. 2:1–4; 3:1–15; 4:20–21, 29–34; 6:1–14; and 11:9–13)

At the time of his death, David admonished Solomon, "Be strong, be courageous, and keep the charge of the LORD your God, walking in his ways and keeping his statutes, . . . as it is written in the law of Moses." Solomon's name means "the LORD's beloved." A review of Solomon's life is mixed with many achievements as well as glaring disappointments. On the one hand, Solomon consolidated the disparate tribes of Israel into a united kingdom, established international trade, and conducted an extensive building program that included an elaborate palace complex and a temple for the Lord in Jerusalem. Solomon was known for his wisdom, which is said to have been greater than "the wisdom of all the people of the east, and all the wisdom of Egypt." On the other hand, Solomon is remembered for many deeds that were not pleasing to God. He married a number of foreign wives, made alliances with enemy nations, used forced labor and taxed the people heavily to build and pay for expensive building projects, and he ceased serving the Lord faithfully as he had been admonished. Solomon established the worship of gods in high places, which led to the decline of the faithful commitment of the people to the Lord their God. Internal dissent and external hostilities led to a schism after Solomon's death, dividing the kingdom into Israel in the north and Judah in the south.

Rehoboam
(1 Kgs. 11:9–13; 11:41–12:19; and 14:21–31)

The name *Rehoboam* means "the people is enlarged." The people, especially those of the northern tribes, were weary of the burdens placed upon them during the reign of Solomon. In an attempt to bring unity and to appease the people of the north, Rehoboam went to Shechem to meet with the leaders, who asked for relief from their heavy taxation. However, before deciding on his response, Rehoboam met with a group of older men, who advised him to be a servant of the people; in so doing, they said, he would win the people's support. He refused to follow their advice. Then he asked counsel of a group of younger men, who advised him to increase the burdens upon the people to keep them under his control. This advice he accepted. The people of the north would not accept his leadership, however. Rehoboam planned to attack the tribes of the north but was warned by the Lord to refrain from that act and to remain in Judah. He obeyed the Lord and did not attack. Rehoboam reigned over the tribes of Benjamin and Judah in the south for seventeen years.

Jeroboam
(1 Kgs. 11:26–40; 12:20, 25–13:34)

Jeroboam I was a servant of Solomon. Prior to Solomon's death, Jeroboam was told by the prophet Ahijah that he would become the ruler of the ten tribes in the north. Solomon heard of Ahijah's words to Jeroboam and sought to kill him. Jeroboam fled to Egypt and returned years later when Rehoboam became king. The people of Israel, the ten tribes of the north, had rejected Rehoboam and then made Jeroboam their king. Jeroboam's reign was filled with abominations. He made two calves of gold and established altars in Bethel and Dan where the gods of gold were worshiped. An unnamed prophet confronted Jeroboam with words from the Lord that what he had done was evil and declared what God would do to punish Jeroboam and the people. This was the beginning of the fall of the northern kingdom of Israel that would occur many years later after a succession of mostly unworthy and unfaithful kings.

Elijah
(1 Kgs. 18:1–19:21)

During the reigns of Ahab and Ahaziah, kings of Israel in the north in the ninth century BCE, there appeared a prophet, Elijah. In this section we will focus only on one of the stories of Elijah. His challenge to the priests of Baal on Mount Carmel is one of the most dramatic stories in the whole Old Testament. With God's power and presence working through him, Elijah was able to prove that the Lord is God and not Baal. After he won the contest on Mount Carmel, Elijah killed the priests of Baal. Then the king's wife, Jezebel, ordered Elijah caught and killed. He fled to the wilderness, where, after a time of doubt and testing, in the stillness of a quiet whisper, he is assured of God's presence. Elijah, one of the few faithful persons in all of the northern kingdom, becomes a symbol of faithfulness for God's people for the centuries that follow. Because he did not die but was taken up into heaven, the faithful believed that he would one day return (see Mal. 4:5).

Hezekiah
(2 Kgs. 18:1–8; 19:1–19, 32–36; and 20:1–21)

Two kings of the southern kingdom of Judah are especially noteworthy: Hezekiah and Josiah. Hezekiah reigned for twenty-nine years in Jerusalem, and it is said of him, "He did what was right in the sight of the LORD. . . . There was no one like him among all the kings of Judah." Hezekiah brought great reform in religious matters and returned the people to the worship of the one true God. In the first month of his reign he reopened the doors of the temple in Jerusalem and reinstituted traditional worship in the house of the Lord. He removed the idols in the high places and reestablished trust in the Lord God among the people. During his reign, Judah faced many threats from hostile armies, but Hezekiah prevailed upon the people to trust in God and not in alliances with other nations. Hezekiah became critically ill but prayed to God for healing and his prayers were answered. The prophet Isaiah delivered a message to Hezekiah that Judah would one day fall to the Babylonians and her people would be taken into captivity.

Josiah
(2 Kgs. 22:1–23:25)

Josiah became the sixteenth king of Judah when he was only eight years old, and he served in that role for thirty-one years. He is the second of the prominent, faithful kings of Judah and, like Hezekiah, was a reformer. His reforms were even more extensive than his predecessor's. Josiah initiated a restoration of the temple in order to return it to the holy place it was built to be. In the process of the restoration, a book of the law was found and the words were read to Josiah. He asked the prophetess Huldah the meaning of the words, and she interpreted to Josiah the law of the Lord. Josiah made a covenant with God and instituted major reforms in response to the teachings of the law. He deposed the idolatrous priests, confiscated the idols and beat them into dust, removed the altars to foreign gods and broke them into pieces, and restored true worship in the temple. He commanded the people to keep the Passover of the Lord as prescribed in the book of the covenant, a festival that had not been kept since the days of the judges. Josiah was killed in battle at Megiddo while seeking to protect his people from Pharaoh Neco.

Ezra
(Ezra 1:1–7; 7:1–10, 27–28; 8:21–23 and Neh. 8:1–12)

Israel had fallen to the Assyrians in 722 BCE, and in 587 BCE, the Babylonians captured Judah. Many of the people of Judah were taken captive to Babylon, where they remained in exile for more than fifty years. The Persians, who looked favorably upon the Jews, then conquered the Babylonians. The Jews were allowed to return to Judah to reclaim and occupy their homeland. Ezra was a scribe and priest who was commissioned by the king of Persia to return with the people to bring order in the new community. He assumed civil and religious authority and was given funds for the rebuilding of the temple. Ezra opposed the practice of men marrying women of foreign heritage because he feared the influence of pagan women on their husbands. So he commanded them to divorce their wives and marry Jewish women. The tradition surrounding Ezra is that he was a great translator and interpreter of the books of the Law. During the time of Ezra, the people were led in a great religious revival that culminated in the Festival of Booths, which commemorated God's deliverance of the people from bondage in Egypt and sustaining them through their years in the wilderness.

Nehemiah
(Neh. 1:1–2:8; 5:14–19; and 7:73b–8:18)

Nehemiah was a servant of the Persian king Artaxerxes. Nehemiah had learned of the deplorable conditions of his people in Judah and its capital city, Jerusalem. He came to God with a very moving prayer of confession and petition (see 1:4–11). His prayer was answered, and the king granted him permission to return to Judah. Nehemiah was appointed governor of the territory. Upon his return, he set about gathering workers to rebuild the walls of the city. This task met considerable resistance from a variety of enemies, so the laborers worked with a tool in one hand and a weapon in the other. In a very dramatic event, the people were assembled to hear the reading of the law of Moses (see 7:73b–8:12). Ezra, the priest, read the words of the law, and the Levites interpreted the meaning of the words. The people responded with praise and thanksgiving to God and with commitment to serve the Lord. This was also the occasion for reinstituting the Festival of Booths, commemorating their journey of deliverance through the wilderness.

Timeline of Period from Moses to Nehemiah

Dates BCE	Key Events and Persons
c. 1290	Exodus from Egypt, led by Moses
c. 1290–1250	Wilderness wanderings
c. 1250	Entrance into Canaan under leadership of Joshua
c. 1250–1020	Period of the judges (including Deborah, Gideon, and Samson)
c. 1020–1000	Samuel and the reign of King Saul
c. 1000–961	Reign of King David (Jonathan and Nathan)
c. 961–922	Reign of King Solomon
922	Death of Solomon and the division of the kingdom into north and south
722	Fall of Israel, the northern kingdom, to Assyria
587	Fall of Judah, the southern kingdom, to Babylonia
593–539	Babylonian exile
c. 538	Beginning of the return of the exiles to Jerusalem
520–515	Rebuilding of the temple (Ezra and Nehemiah)

Note: Dates in BCE move chronologically from larger to smaller numbers.

This timeline is based upon one in Bernhard W. Anderson, *Understanding the Old Testament*, 3d ed., (Englewood Cliffs, N.J.: Prentice-Hall, 1975).

Chapter Six

The Books of the Prophets

In chapter 5 we saw that the Hebrew Scriptures were written over many centuries and were gathered into three collections: The Law, The Prophets, and The Writings. The Prophets are divided into the Former Prophets, which include the books of history, and the Latter Prophets, which include what we usually think of as the books of the prophets. The books of the Latter Prophets are divided into two sections: the Major Prophets, which include Isaiah, Jeremiah, and Ezekiel, and the Minor Prophets, which include the twelve shorter books. The designation of "Major" and "Minor" is misleading, suggesting that some are more important than others. Those books included in the Major Prophets are simply longer and were written on separate scrolls. The Minor Prophets are shorter and were joined together on one scroll. Thus, "Major" and "Minor" have nothing to do with significance but with the length of the manuscripts.

In this chapter we will comment briefly on seven of the books of the prophets. A dominant theme in all of the prophets is a concern for justice and righteousness, for living according to the commandments of the Lord and being faithful to the covenant made between God and the people. Also, each prophet brings God's judgment upon the people for their failures to live according to the law.

Prayer Prompted by Scripture

Each of the prophets, in his own setting and style, proclaimed God's word in calling the people to a life of righteousness and justice. When we turn to Psalms we find in many of them this same concern for righteousness and justice. The psalmist reminds the people again and again that God's favor is extended to the lowly and the needy: the widow, the orphan, the oppressed, the poor, the prisoners, and many others who are victims of one circumstance or another. To be righteous and just, from the psalmist's perspective, is to be in faithful, obedient relationship with God and to have compassion toward those for whom God has compassion. That message is similar to what the prophets proclaim. As you begin your study of the prophets, meditate upon the words of Psalm 146. Notice especially: (1) the relationship between persons and God, (2) those to whom God's favor, or advocacy, is expressed, and (3) how God cares for those in need.

Praise the LORD!
Praise the LORD, O my soul!
I will praise the LORD as long as I live;
  I will sing praises to my God all my life long.

Do not put your trust in princes,
  in mortals, in whom there is no help.
When their breath departs, they return to the earth;
  on that very day their plans perish.

Happy are those whose help is the God of Jacob,
  whose hope is in the LORD their God,
who made heaven and earth,
  the sea, and all that is in them;
who keeps faith forever;
  who executes justice for the oppressed;
  who gives food to the hungry.

The LORD sets the prisoners free;
  the LORD opens the eyes of the blind.
The LORD lifts up those who are bowed down;
  the LORD loves the righteous.
The LORD watches over the strangers;
  he upholds the orphan and the widow,
  but the way of the wicked he brings to ruin.

The LORD will reign forever,
  your God, O Zion, for all generations.
Praise the LORD!

Reflect on Psalm 146 by considering several questions and doing a brief activity.

On what does the believer base her or his hope? What is not dependable?

What is the nature of God's justice?

What is required to be righteous?

Make a list of the eight categories of persons who are recipients of God's favor.

Identify what God does on behalf of those eight different groups of people.

Prophets and Prophecy

There is a common misconception about prophets and prophecy. We often think a prophet is one who foretells the future and that prophecy is a matter of special knowledge about what will occur. The true prophet was one who had a very special relationship with God, who understood clearly God's commandments and the consequences of not obeying those commandments. The prophets were persons whose faith and courage motivated them to speak God's word to the people, to call them to repentance and renewal of their covenant relationship with God, and who warned them about what would happen if they continued to sin and go their evil ways. The prophets were more *forthtellers* of God's word and will than they were *foretellers* of future events.

The timeline and list of kings and prophets on page 59 will help you see the setting in which each appeared. Let us now consider seven of the prophets, with brief descriptions regarding the time, place, and message of each one. The seven are: Isaiah, Jeremiah, Ezekiel, Hosea, Amos, Jonah, and Micah.

Isaiah

Read 6:1–8 (the call of Isaiah); 7:10–17 (a sign from the Lord); 9:1–7 (the people who walked in darkness); 22:1–25 (warning of destruction); 39:1–8 (envoys from Babylon); 40:1–11, 27–31 (words of hope); 52:13–53:12 (the suffering servant); and 62:1–12 (return to Jerusalem).

The book of Isaiah is a composite of writings from three different time periods. The first section, chapters 1–39, was written from the perspective of a people living in Jerusalem prior to their exile to Babylon. In Hebrew, the name *Isaiah* means "the Lord has saved." Isaiah 1:1 records this period of Isaiah's work as spanning the reigns of four kings: Uzziah, Jotham, Ahaz, and Hezekiah. In

Isaiah 6:1–18, we read the story of Isaiah's call by God while he was worshiping in the temple. He was overwhelmed by the glory and majesty of God and realized how sinful he was. He experienced absolution of his sin and then was given the power to speak God's message to the people. Isaiah spoke many words of judgment against the people for having forsaken the faith of their ancestors who trusted in God to deliver them, and instead putting their trust in idols and false gods and in their own abilities to protect and defend themselves.

There are words of hope (see 7:10–14 and 9:2–7) in this section, as the prophet expects the coming of one who would deliver the people from their enemies. These passages are often used during the season of Advent in anticipation of the coming of the Messiah. However, most of this section of Isaiah is a series of oracles and pronouncements against the cities, regions, and nations who have forsaken the Lord God.

The second section, chapters 40–55, reflects a very different time and theme. Whereas the first section was written in a time of great turmoil with the threat of destruction and captivity, this section was written in the midst of the exile in Babylon and contains many expressions of hope and promise for a new day when God would reestablish the people of Israel in the land promised to them long ago. Also in this section there are four passages identified as "servant songs," which refer to one who would come as the servant of the Lord to save the people. From a Christian perspective, after the life, death, and resurrection of Jesus, he is the one who is believed to have fulfilled this role of the suffering servant.

The third section, chapters 56–66, was written from the perspective of a people who had resettled in Judah and Jerusalem following their time of exile in Babylon. There are references to work already having begun on restoring the temple (61:1–4) and reestablishing the worship of the Lord, the God of Abraham, Isaac, and Jacob. There are warnings and judgments in this section, but there is also the strong promise that once again Jerusalem will be called "the City of the LORD, the Zion of the Holy One of Israel" (60:14).

Jeremiah

Read 1:1–10 (his call); 7:1–28 (speaking the word of the Lord); 18:1–12 (parable of the potter); 26:1–15 (Jeremiah on trial); 31:31–34 (the new covenant); and 39:1–18 (people captured, Jeremiah protected).

The name *Jeremiah* means "the Lord hurls" which seems very appropriate in the sense of his hurling the word of the Lord to the people of Judah. Jeremiah's call by God to be the Lord's prophet came when he was a boy, and he resisted by saying that he was too young to be a prophet. The Lord countered the excuse by declaring that he was not too young. The Lord touched his lips and put the word of the Lord in his mouth. Jeremiah served as a prophet for about forty years, beginning with the reign of King Josiah and concluding with the last king of Judah, Zedekiah, at the time of the fall of Jerusalem to the invading armies of Babylon in 586 BCE.

Jeremiah carried a heavy burden. He understood well the requirements of the covenant: that the people were expected to worship God and God only and were to live as a righteous and just people. But they worshiped foreign gods, they did not obey the commandments, and they forgot their special relationship with the One who delivered them from Egypt and brought them to the Promised Land. It was Jeremiah's responsibility to proclaim the word of the Lord to the people, to bring judgment upon their evil ways, and to declare that it was God's plan that they would be taken into captivity by the Babylonians. For proclaiming God's message, Jeremiah was charged with treason, jailed, and threatened with death. As one would expect, this caused him to come to God with great despair and discouragement. However, God sustained him throughout his days.

In addition to words of judgment and doom, Jeremiah offered some words of hope. Jeremiah 31:31–34 speaks of a new covenant and is one of the most memorable passages in the whole Old Testament. The prophet also offered words of promise that God would not abandon the people completely but only for a time. Judah was conquered by the invading armies of Babylon, and the people were taken into captivity. Jeremiah did not go to Babylon with his fellow citizens but stayed on in Jerusalem for a time and then went to Egypt, where presumably he died, though there is no record of that.

Ezekiel

Read 1:1–3 (setting is in exile); 1:28b–3:15 (Ezekiel's call); 24:15–27 (death of his wife); 34:1–24 (the shepherds of Israel); 36:16–38 (restoration of the people in Jerusalem); and 37:1–14 (valley of dry bones).

The book of Ezekiel is a long, dynamic, dramatic, and complicated book. Hebrew tradition taught that only a mature person was to read the book, which meant one had to be thirty years old. Ezekiel contains a variety of types of writings: oracles, symbolic actions, visions, allegories, prophetic proclamations, and priestly vocabulary. This book is unique in that it is the only one of all the books of the prophets that is written entirely in the first person. In the opening verses of the book, we learn that Ezekiel is a priest living in exile with those who were among the first to be deported from Jerusalem in 597 BCE with King Jehoiachin and other prominent citizens of Judah. It is unusual that Ezekiel, a priest of the temple, would also be called by God to be a prophet, but that is what we read in chapters 2 and 3. A moving passage is in chapter 24, where Ezekiel's wife dies and Ezekiel is told by God not to mourn her death but to act normal. This would be a sign of how God would respond to the "death" of the holy city and temple and the people of the covenant.

Throughout the book a statement is repeated over and over again: "The word of the LORD came to me: You, O mortal, thus says the Lord GOD to the land of Israel." In the NRSV, the Hebrew word *adam,* which means "the man" or "the human," is translated as "Mortal," but in other translations it appears as "Son of man." The word appears ninety-three times in the book and is meant to emphasize the humanity of the one called by God to proclaim the word of the Lord.

The first thirty-two chapters of the book are mostly words of judgment against the people for their sin of profaning the holy temple, for depending upon other nations for their security instead of on the Lord God, for not obeying the commandments, and for forsaking their covenant relationship with God. This is Ezekiel's way of explaining to the people the reasons for the calamities that have happened to them: the destruction of their temple, their military defeat, and their being taken into captivity. The last chapters of the book contain more words of hope and encouragement to prepare for the day of their return to the land promised to them by God and for the time of rebuilding their lives as well as the temple. A familiar and poignant passage is the allegory of the valley of dry bones (37:1–14), which suggests new life will emerge from that which appeared to be dead. *Ezekiel* in Hebrew means "God will strengthen."

Hosea

Read 1:1–11 (marriage to Gomer and three children); 2:16–4:10 (metaphor of unfaithful wife); and 11:1–12:6 (God's love will prevail).

Hosea was the only one of the prophets who was a native of the northern kingdom, Israel, and his ministry of thirty years was directed solely to that realm. Hosea's name in Hebrew means "deliverance." A major theme of the book revolves around the metaphor of a faithful husband married to an adulterous wife. Hosea marries Gomer, a prostitute, who gives birth to two sons and a daughter whose names have symbolic meaning in terms of God's actions in the life of the people.[1] His relationship with Gomer is like God's relationship with the people of Israel. They, like Gomer, have prostituted themselves before Baal, the god of the Canaanites, who is believed to bring rain and therefore an abundance of crops. The people would be dismissed from God's presence because of their unfaithfulness, just as Hosea is told by God to rid himself of Gomer.

The sinfulness of Gomer and Israel and their rejection by Hosea and God, respectively, is not the whole story. God forgives the people of Israel and offers to be their "husband" again if they respond in faithfulness. Just so, Hosea is instructed to reclaim Gomer from her promiscuous life and to live with her in love and forgiveness. We see this metaphor expressed in chapters 2 and 3 and also in chapter 11, which includes loving, compassionate words that reveal the

1. First son, Jezreel, meaning "God sows," daughter, Lo-ruhamah, meaning "not pitied," the second son, Lo-ammi, meaning "not my people."

nature of God's relationship with the people of Israel. Even though Israel has lived the life of the harlot, God is willing to receive her back into a relationship if only she will be faithful.

The book of Hosea is in two parts: Chapters 1–3 are a narrative, with the remaining eleven chapters being speeches of the prophet. The narrative describes Hosea's life with Gomer and God's relationship with Israel. The speeches are all words of the Lord delivered to the people of Israel. They are mostly words of judgment, but words of hope and promise appear in several places. In the last eleven chapters of the book, we read the word *Ephraim* many, many times. Ephraim was one of the twelve tribes who settled in the north. The tribe of Ephraim came to prominence and for Hosea represented the whole of the kingdom of Israel.

Amos

Read 1:1–2 (historical context); 2:5–11 (judgment against Israel); 5:21–24 (call for justice and righteousness); 7:10–17 (the only narrative); and 9:11–15 (words of hope and promise).

In just a few verses (1:1 and 7:10–17) we learn that the prophet Amos lived in Tekoa, a town in Judah south of Jerusalem, where he was a keeper of flocks and a "dresser of sycamore trees." The name *Amos,* in Hebrew means "burden bearer." He prophesied during the reigns of Uzziah in Judah and Jeroboam II in Israel. He delivered the word of the Lord to the people of Israel at Bethel and Samaria in the north even though he lived in the south. This period of time was relatively stable in that there were no enemies threatening the borders of either Judah or Israel. It was a time of prosperity, with many people becoming very wealthy at the expense of the poor and disenfranchised.

The people in Israel maintained the pretense of worshiping God, but their worship was contrived and without substance because it had no effect on the way they lived and treated their fellow Jews. Amos saw through the hypocrisy of their worship and delivered a harsh message. This passage, Amos 5:21–24, is the most familiar of the whole book: "I hate, I despise your festivals, and I take no delight in your solemn assemblies. . . . Take away from me the noise of your songs. . . . But let justice roll down like waters, and righteousness like an everflowing stream." Amos is known as the prophet of social justice and has served as an inspiration for those who have sought justice in every generation since.

The opening two chapters include a series of judgments against the nations and Israel. It is an interesting sequence of judgments and follows a similar pattern in each. Amos starts with Damascus to the northeast, followed by Gaza to the southwest, then Tyre to the northwest, then Edom and Moab to the east and southeast. The judgments against them are because of their offenses against their neighbors. People in Israel could agree with such judgments against their enemies. However, Amos sneaks up on them by bringing judgment against Judah to the south and then zeroes in with strong words of condemnation from the Lord against the so-called religious people of Israel. They are accused of grave injustices against the righteous and the poor. Though Amos has been called a prophet of doom, there are words of hope and promise in the last chapter of the book, in which God promises to "restore the fortunes of my people Israel."

Jonah

Read all four chapters.

The book of Jonah is different from all of the other books of the prophets. First of all, it is very difficult to place the prophet in any specific historical context since no kings or special events are mentioned within the book. Second, it reads more like a parable or story than it does as prophecy. All of the other prophetic books present oracles, judgments, and prophecies in almost every chapter; whereas in Jonah there is only one sentence of prophecy: "Forty days more, and Nineveh shall be overthrown" (3:4b). Third, in Jonah the people hear and believe the prophet's warnings rather than turning a deaf ear as the people do to all the other prophets.

The story of Jonah is familiar because of Jonah's being swallowed by a big fish and spewed up three days later following his prayer of lament and petition to God. Whether or not it is possible for a man to be swallowed by a big fish and survive for three days makes for interesting speculation, but totally misses the point of the story. The message of the book conveys several truths: (1) God has a purpose for nations as well as individuals, (2) God's purpose will be fulfilled despite efforts to undermine it, (3) God's grace and mercy are extended to people "outside the fold" as well as to the chosen ones, and (4) God is Lord of all creation.

Jonah is called by God to deliver a message to the people of Nineveh, a city east of Israel in Assyria, but he refuses by boarding a ship headed for Tarshish, which is across the Mediterranean Sea in the opposite direction. The storm and the great fish are devices in the story to show that God is in control. Jonah is given a second chance to take God's message to Nineveh and he does so, very successfully. The king and the people believe his message, repent of their sins, and are forgiven by God. Jonah is angry with God and ends up pouting under a tree that dies in the hot sun, which makes him even angrier with God. The book ends with an unanswered question spoken by the Lord: "Should I not be concerned about Nineveh, that great city, in which there are more than a hundred and twenty thousand persons who do not know their right hand from their left, and also many animals?" (4:11).

Micah

Read 1:1 (the setting); 2:1–13 (a remnant shall return); 3:9–4:5 (swords into plowshares); 5:2–5a (expecting a shepherd king to lead the people); and 6:6–8 (what the Lord requires).

Despite the fact that the prophet Micah grew up in Moresheth, a small, rural, Judean village southeast of Jerusalem, he never flinched from proclaiming the word of the Lord in the capital cities of Israel and Judah. His service as a prophet occurred during the reigns of Jotham, Ahaz, and Hezekiah in Judah, and he lived to witness the fall of the northern kingdom of Israel. The book is composed of two kinds of speeches.[2] In his *judgment speeches,* Micah declares that the people will be punished for their acts of injustice against their neighbors (2:1–9). His message is somewhat similar to that of Amos and Hosea. Micah warned the priests, the prophets, and the rulers of Judah that if they did not change their ways they would suffer the same consequences as their kinfolk in the north (3:11–12)—that is, they would be conquered and taken into captivity. In his *salvation speeches,* Micah offers words of hope. He speaks words of the Lord promising that a remnant of the faithful will be saved (2:12–13 and 7:18) and that a new kind of ruler will come forth from Bethlehem to bring peace and security to the people (5:2–5). Two of the more familiar passages in the Old Testament are found in Micah, both having to do with what is expected of the faithful who would serve the Lord according to the law: "They shall beat their swords into plowshares, and their spears into pruning hooks" (4:3) and "What does the LORD require of you but to do justice, and to love kindness, and to walk humbly with your God?" (6:8). The name *Micah* in Hebrew means "who is like the Lord," which is not a question but a statement.

2. These two types of prophetic speeches are described in the introductory article to Micah in *The Access Bible,* NRSV, (New York: Oxford University Press, 1999)

Kings and Prophets of Israel and Judah

	Northern Kingdom (Israel)		**Southern Kingdom (Judah)**		
930 B.C.E.	Jeroboam I	(22 years)	Rehoboam	(17 years)	
	Nadab	(2)	Abijah	(3)	
	Baasha	(24)	Asa	(41)	
	Elah	(2)			
	Zimri	(7 days)			
	Omri	(12)			
	Ahab	(22)	Jehoshaphat	(25)	
850	Ahaziah	(2)			
	Jehoram	(12)	Jehoram	(8)	
	Jehu	(28)	Ahaziah	(1)	
			Athaliah	(7)	
810	Jehoahaz	(17)	Joash	(40)	
	Jehoash	(16)			
AMOS	Jeroboam II	(41)	Amaziah	(29)	
	Zechariah	(6 mos.)	Uzziah	(52)	**ISAIAH (I)**
	Shallum	(1 mo.)			
	Menahem	(10)			
HOSEA	Pekahiah	(2)			
	Pekah	(20)	Jotham	(16)	
	Hoshea	(9)	Ahaz	(16)	**MICAH**
722	**Fall of the northern kingdom**		Hezekiah	(29)	
			Manasseh	(55)	
			Amon	(2)	
			Josiah	(31)	**JEREMIAH**
			Jehoahaz	(3 mos.)	**ZEPHANIAH**
			Jehoiakim	(11)	**HABAKKUK**
			Jehoiachin	(3 mos.)	
			Zedekiah	(11)	
586			**Fall of Judah**		**OBADIAH**
	Exile in Babylon				**EZEKIEL**
					ISAIAH (II)
538	First exiles return (Zerubbabel)				**HAGGAI**
458	Second group returns (Ezra)				
					ZECHARIAH
432	Last group of exiles returns (Nehemiah)				**ISAIAH (III)**
					MALACHI

No dates can be confirmed for:

JOEL (probably during the exile)
JONAH
NAHUM

A Map of Israel and Judah

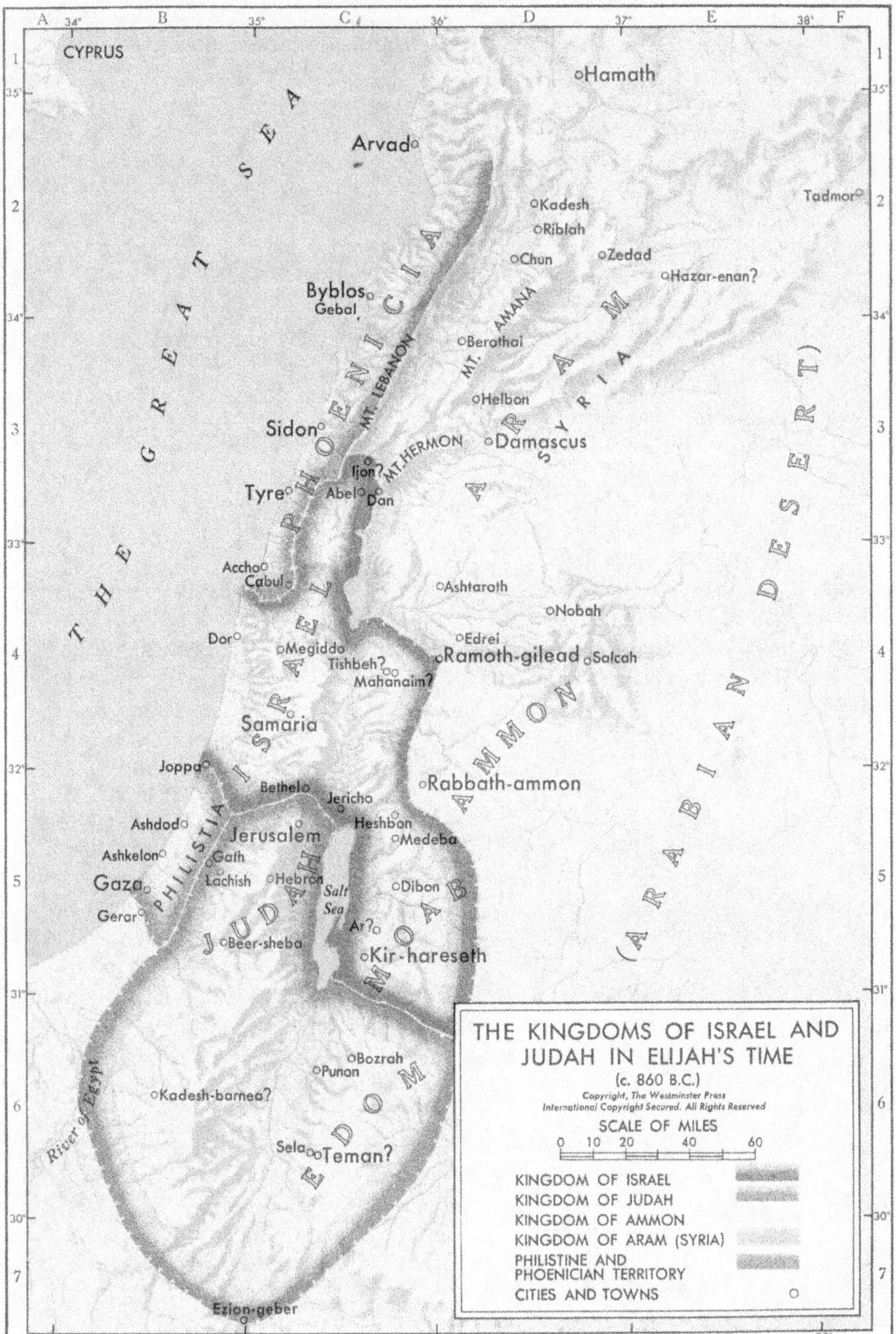

Chapter Seven
The Books of the Writings

We now come to the conclusion of our brief overview of the Old Testament. In this chapter we will explore the third collection of the Hebrew Scriptures, called The Writings. This collection of books in the Hebrew Scriptures is presented in a different order than in the Christian Scriptures. The Writings were collected over several centuries and were accepted officially in the Jewish canon in the late first century CE. The books included in The Writings represent several different types of literature. Psalms is composed of songs, prayers, and poems. Proverbs is mostly a collection of wise sayings. Ruth and Esther are more like historical fiction. Job is an extended dialogue between God, Satan, Job, and three friends. Daniel is an example of apocalyptic writing. In the Old Testament, the books of The Writings appear amidst books that we often think of as history or prophecy.

Prayer Prompted by Scripture

We have begun each of the previous six chapters with a psalm as the focus for our praying. We have seen how these ancient words have relevance to our faith and life today. As we conclude our overview of the Old Testament, spend a few minutes with the most familiar psalm of all, Psalm 23. First, read the words below from the NRSV translation. Then reflect briefly upon several questions. Conclude your time with Psalm 23 by reading the words again in the Contemporary English Version. If you have one or two other translations available, you will find inspiration from reading Psalm 23 from them as well.

The LORD is my shepherd, I shall not want.
He makes me lie down in green pastures;
he leads me beside still waters;
he restores my soul.
He leads me in right paths
for his name's sake.

Even though I walk through the darkest valley,
I fear no evil;
for you are with me;
your rod and your staff—
they comfort me.

You prepare a table before me
in the presence of my enemies;
you anoint my head with oil;
my cup overflows.
Surely goodness and mercy shall follow me
all the days of my life,
and I shall dwell in the house of the LORD
my whole life long.

Consider the following questions as you meditate upon these words of the psalmist. Reflect on the questions in a prayerful, thoughtful way. It may be helpful to close your eyes as you meditate or to have quiet music playing in the background.

What memories from childhood, or even more recent times, come to you when you read or hear the words of Psalm 23?

When have the words of the psalm been most comforting and meaningful to you?

What is the darkest valley you have experienced and known that God was with you?

In what right paths do you pray God will lead you in this time of your life?

Psalm 23 from the CEV:

You, LORD, are my shepherd. I will never be in need.
    You let me rest in fields of green grass.
You lead me to streams of peaceful water, and you refresh my life.
    You are true to your name, and you lead me along right paths.
I may walk through valleys as dark as death, but I won't be afraid.
    You are with me, and your shepherd's rod makes me feel safe.
You treat me to a feast, while my enemies watch.
    You honor me as your guest, and you fill my cup until it overflows.
Your kindness and love will always be with me each day of my life,
    and I will live forever in your house, LORD.

Summaries of the Books in The Writings

These brief summaries of each of the books are presented in the order that they appear in the Christian Bible. When you look at the table of contents in your Bible, you will see that these books are scattered throughout. Ruth, 1 and 2 Chronicles, Ezra, Nehemiah, and Esther are grouped with the historical writings. Lamentations and Daniel are grouped with the prophets, leaving the others in a group that we identify as the books of Wisdom.

Ruth

(Read the whole book of Ruth.)

In the Christian Scriptures the book of Ruth follows the book of Judges, which is understandable considering that the first verse reads, "In the days when the judges ruled . . . ." At first glance it appears to be a book of history related to the time of the judges. However, in the Hebrew Scriptures the book is in the collection of The Writings, clustered with Esther, Ecclesiastes, and the Song of Solomon, which are read during particular Jewish festivals. Bible scholars have differences of opinion regarding the date and setting of its origin. Based upon the genealogy in the last three verses of the book, some suggest it was written in a time near the reign of King David. Others suggest its origin is in the time of Ezra and Nehemiah and that it serves as a counterweight to the hostility toward intermarriage expressed in these two books.

Ruth is a dramatic and beautiful story of the devotion of a young woman to the people of her mother-in-law. Ruth was a Moabite woman and her mother-in-law was of the people of Israel. Independent of the time of its origin, the book of Ruth teaches several important truths about God and the relationship between God and people. God's purposes are fulfilled in surprising and unexpected ways. God's love and grace are extended to all people whether or not they are included among the chosen nation. When people are faithful in their relationships with God and with other people, they receive blessings from God.

First and Second Chronicles

The Chronicles were written after the return from exile to give encouragement to the people of Israel as they resettled in the land of promise. The first nine chapters of 1 Chronicles contain nothing but genealogical lists. The historical narrative begins with the death of Saul and the reign of King David. David is the key figure in 1 Chronicles, which emphasizes his successful exploits and actions. David is presented in a very positive light, with no mention of his affair with Bathsheba, his arranging for the death of Uriah, or his encounter with the prophet Nathan.

Second Chronicles begins with the reign of Solomon and features his role in building the temple and establishing temple worship as a central part of the life of the people. Solomon's unfaithfulness in pursuing foreign gods is omitted. Other kings who played a positive, important role in Judah are presented briefly, including Asa, Jehoshaphat, Hezekiah, and Josiah. Chronicles presents these kings as well as David and Solomon as exemplary role models for those who would lead the people of Israel after their return from captivity in Babylon.

Ezra and Nehemiah

We have already dealt with these two books in chapter 5. In the Christian Bible, Ezra and Nehemiah are seen as part of the collection of historical books.

Esther

(Read the whole book of Esther.)

The setting of the story of Esther is in the foreign land of Persia. There are four main characters in the story: the king (called Ahasuerus but associated with Xerxes), Haman (an official in the king's court and a prototypical villain), Esther (a Jewish woman and the heroine), and Mordecai (Esther's cousin who cared for her after the death of her father and mother). The story is full of intrigue, centering around Haman's plot to have all the Jews killed. Queen Esther, whose identity as a Jew is not known, finds favor with the king. Encouraged by Mordecai, Esther reveals her identity to the king and prevails upon him to spare the Jews. This in turn causes the downfall of Haman. The story of Esther is read during the Jewish festival of Purim, when a festive meal is shared and gifts are exchanged. One interesting feature is that the name of God is not mentioned once in the whole book, which is unusual since it is the faith of Esther and Mordecai in God that brings victory from imminent death.

Job

(Job is long; just skim the book in order to gain a sense of the outline.)

The book of Job focuses on a single question: "If God is in control of everything and is just, why do good people suffer?" The story begins with Job (rhymes with *robe*) being described as a righteous man. He is "blameless and upright, one who feared God and turned away from evil" (1:1). In a conversation, Satan (in Hebrew the name means "the accuser") says to God that Job would not be righteous if he were not so prosperous. If he were to suffer, then he would curse God. God allows Satan to bring calamities against Job so that he loses everything and is stricken with a dreaded disease. In the midst of his calamity Job laments to God but continues to be faithful. He is visited by three friends who in a series of three speeches try to convince Job that he has sinned and that that is the reason he is suffering. Job maintains his innocence but not without lamenting to God and asking for God's explanation of why he has suffered so much. Job is reminded that it is God who is in control of all that exists. The story has a happy ending, with Job's fortune being restored to him and increased fourfold. The beginning and ending of the book are in a prose style, while the bulk of the book—the dialogues between Job and his three friends—is in the form of poetry.

Psalms

(Read passages suggested in the text below.)

Psalms is probably the most familiar of all the books in The Writings. Psalms was the first prayer book of the Jewish people and is to this day a prayer book of God's people in synagogues, churches, chapels, and cathedrals. The Hebrew title for the book is *tehillim,* meaning "songs of praise." The English title, Psalms, is derived from the Greek word *psalmos,* a translation of the Hebrew word *mismor,* which appears in the preface of fifty-seven psalms in the form of "A psalm [or *psalmos,* or *mismor*] of David." The word *psalmos* means "a song sung to the accompaniment of stringed instruments."

Psalms is a collection of 150 hymns, prayers, and poems, many of which are attributed to King David. Many different persons or groups composed the psalms. The collection of psalms is divided into five different books of unequal length with no clear rationale for the division.[1] One possible explanation for five

1. Book 1 (Ps. 1–41); Book 2 (Ps. 42–72); Book 3 (Ps. 73–89); Book 4 (Ps. 90–106); and Book 5 (Ps. 107–150).

books of psalms is that David, seen as almost equal to Moses in the tradition of the people of Israel, must have five books attributed to him to be like Moses, who tradition taught was the author of the Pentateuch.

Within the 150 psalms there are many different types of writing that are categorized in a variety of ways by the many interpreters of Psalms. We will not go into detail on this matter, but we can look at some examples. The most prevalent type of psalm is the laments, of which there are between sixty and seventy. There are *personal laments,* in which an individual comes before God with grief, distress, anger, or sorrow (see Ps. 22). Other psalms are *corporate laments,* in which the psalmist expresses anger, frustration, and despair to God on behalf of the whole community (see Ps. 60). A second type is *psalms of praise*. These psalms are expressions of praise and thanksgiving to the Lord for God's mighty works of creation, deliverance, and mercy (see Ps. 111). *Psalms of trust* are prayers expressing confidence, faith, and hope in God's presence and power to protect and care for the person (see Ps. 62). *Salvation history psalms* summarize God's mighty acts in the history of the people of Israel (see Ps. 136). A number of psalms focus on the king of Israel or God as king; these are called *royal psalms* (see Ps. 99).

Several psalms are included in the category of *creation psalms,* which describe and celebrate God's act as creator of all that exists—the universe, nature, animals, and human beings (see Ps. 104). Another type is *psalms of Zion,* which focus on Jerusalem as the holy city and holy mountain (see Ps. 48). Psalm 119 is an acrostic psalm and the longest with 176 verses. It does not fit neatly into any of the above categories so it is treated as its own type, *torah psalm,* which is an affirmation and celebration of the role of the law of God in the life of the people. Categorizing psalms by type in some instances is arbitrary and depends upon the criteria one uses to determine the categories. Many psalms may contain elements of more than one type. Another way to group the psalms is to place them into just two categories: those that *speak about* God and those that are prayers *addressed to* God. All of those psalms that are prayers addressed to God have the potential to become our prayers as we come into God's presence in times of worship, meditation, and prayer.

Every one of the 150 psalms is written in the form of a poem. Even if there were no verse designations, which was the case for many centuries, it would be clear where the beginnings and endings of the verses are. Hebrew poetry does not follow a pattern with which we are familiar, where words at the end of one or more lines rhyme with words of another line. Rather, in Hebrew poetry the thought or concept of one line or verse "rhymes" with or contrasts with the ideas of another line or verse. This feature of Hebrew poetry is known as *parallelism,* of which there are several types. In *synonymous parallelism,* one line of a verse repeats the thought of the previous line but with different words (see Ps. 27:3). With *synthetic parallelism,* something new is added in the second line to the expression of the first line (see Ps. 27:9). Another type is *comparative parallelism,* in which images or metaphors are used in both lines to compare God's actions or attributes, thus creating little parables (see Ps. 103:11–13). A fourth type is *antithetic parallelism,* in which the thought of the second line contradicts or is opposite to the thought of the preceding line (see Ps. 27:10).

Still another poetic structure is the *acrostic psalm.* It is impossible to recognize an acrostic psalm in English since it only appears as an acrostic in the original Hebrew language. There are twenty-two letters in the Hebrew alphabet, which means in Psalm 25 with its twenty-two verses, each verse begins with a different Hebrew word, with the first letter of each word in the order of the alphabet. In some acrostic psalms, each line or each pair of verses or each verse in a stanza begins with a different letter in the order of the alphabet, such as in Psalm 119.

In many ways, Psalms is the most relevant and contemporary book in the whole Old Testament. It is true that our world is very different from the world of the psalmist in terms of religious practices, social norms, worldview, and all that a modern technological world offers. However, human emotions and relationships are still very much the same. The human experiences of faith, love, joy, hope, despair, sorrow, forgiveness, and all the other emotions are as real to us in our day as they were real for the psalmist in his day. That is one of the reasons many believers turn to the Psalms for comfort in times of sorrow, for support in the times of decision making, and for words of forgiveness in times of confession. See page 71 for some examples of psalms to pray in times of particular needs.

Proverbs

(Read 1:1–7; 3:1–26; 8:1–26; any chapter from 10 to 28; and 31:10–31.)

Proverbs is a difficult book to read straight through, but it is a wonderful book to skim. When you skim through even one chapter, you will discover many wise sayings that are as relevant today as they were the day they were written. The book of Proverbs is composed of several collections of wise teachings and sayings. Proverbs are brief statements of practical wisdom derived from knowing which acts or behaviors of persons bring blessing and reward in contrast to those that cause harm or punishment. Tradition suggests that King Solomon is the source of all the proverbs. It is likely that some of the proverbs originated with Solomon, but there are many other sources, including one collection of thirty sayings (22:17–24:22) from a popular Egyptian wisdom text known as the *Instructions of Amenemope*. The first nine chapters are instructions or speeches of a wise person such as a king, teacher, or father, to a younger person. Each chapter addresses "my child" as the one who must learn how to live in order to be wise, righteous, prosperous, healthy, and secure. Chapters 10–29 (except for the section of Egyptian wisdom identified above) are constructed with two-line pithy sayings, or proverbs. The sayings contrast the wise and the foolish, the righteous and the unrighteous, the rich and the poor, hard work and idleness, joy and sorrow, and hope and fear. The book ends with three independent collections: the Saying of Agur (30:1–33), the Teaching of King Lemuel's Mother (31:1–9) and the Ideal Wife (31:10–31).

Ecclesiastes

(Read 1:1–3:8 and 8:1–9:18.)

The title of the book is derived from the Greek *ekklesia,* which is a translation of the Hebrew word *qual,* meaning "assembly." The one who addresses the assembly is a *Qoheleth* (see 1:1 and the related footnote), which is translated in English as "preacher" (KJV and NIV), "teacher" (NRSV), and "one known to be very wise" (CEV). Like Proverbs, the writer of Ecclesiastes comments on what is known through observing the actions of human beings and the consequences of their actions. Proverbs brings a very positive outlook: The righteous are blessed and the wicked are punished. Ecclesiastes has a very different conclusion: The righteous ones sometimes suffer and sinners sometimes prosper, and whether one is righteous or a sinner the end is the same—death. The refrain, "Vanity of vanities, all is vanity," is repeated several times in the book. The word in Hebrew, *hevel,* means "wind" or "vapor" and suggests that everything is transient, here today and gone tomorrow. The CEV translates the word differently: "Nothing makes sense. Everything is nonsense." Whichever translation you prefer, it is clear that the writer doesn't have a very hopeful or positive outlook on life. He considers what it is that makes life worth living and concludes that neither pleasure, nor wisdom, nor work will bring satisfaction. The most positive aspect of Ecclesiastes is the recognition that one's worth and hope are to be found in God: "Fear God, and keep his commandments; for that is the whole duty of everyone" (12:13). A passage with which you may be familiar begins, "For everything there is a season, and a time for every matter under heaven; a time to be born and a time to die. . . ." (3:1–8). This passage served as the inspiration for a popular song in the 1960s, "Turn, Turn, Turn."

Song of Songs

(Read 1:1–17 and 4:1–16.)

This book has two different titles, Song of Songs and Song of Solomon, and is sometimes referred to as the Song. The book is attributed to Solomon, but most biblical scholars believe that it was written many centuries after Solomon. The Song is a love poem in which two lovers, a man and a woman, and their friends speak to and about each other. The name of God is not mentioned once in the whole book, and for that and other reasons there were many debates over the years whether or not the book should be included in the canon. The Song has been interpreted in several ways: (1) a description of a wedding between Solomon and a woman, (2) as an allegory describing the love relationship between God and the people of Israel, and (3) as a secular love poem with similarities to Egyptian, Arabic, and Syrian love poetry. It is believed to have been included in the canon of the Hebrew Scriptures because of its allegorical nature. For Christians it became an allegory of Christ, the bridegroom, and his bride, the church. Most biblical scholars assert that it is at root a secular love poem.

Lamentations

(Read 1:1–22 and 5:1–22.)

The book of Lamentations is often attributed to Jeremiah, based upon the title "Lamentations of Jeremiah" in the Septuagint, the Greek translation of the Hebrew Scriptures. However, there is nothing in the Hebrew text to confirm that Jeremiah wrote the book. It was more likely written by someone who remained in Jerusalem after the king, the leaders, and the wealthy were all taken into captivity to Babylon. The descriptions of the destruction, desolation, and cruel conditions of the city are so vivid that only an eyewitness could have written the book. (To lament is to grieve, to complain, and to express feelings of abandonment and anger.) The five chapters of Lamentations are a series of five poems. The first four chapters are acrostic poems, with each verse or set of three verses (notice that chapters 1, 2, and 4 have twenty-two verses and chapter 3 has sixty-six verses) beginning with one of the twenty-two letters of the Hebrew alphabet, in alphabetical order. The fifth chapter has twenty-two verses, but it is not an acrostic. It is only possible to see the acrostic structure of the poems in Hebrew or in an English version if the Hebrew characters are printed with their respective verses. The five chapters include nothing of the particular events, characters, or circumstances associated with the defeat of Judah and the destruction of Jerusalem and the temple. However, the chapters are full of the heavy emotions of sadness and despair associated with the events. The writer believes God has punished the people for their great sin but also believes that the innocent should not suffer so greatly. Though the book is filled with despair and disillusionment, there are a few glimmers of hope (as seen in 3:22–33). The book ends with a prayer of petition that God will restore the people to their relationship with God as in the days of old.

Daniel

(Read 1:1–21; 3:1–30; 6:1–28; and 11:2–45.)

Daniel is the only example in the Hebrew Scriptures of apocalyptic writing. A more familiar example of this type of writing is Revelation in the New Testament. The word *apocalypse* is derived from a Greek word, *apokalypsis,* meaning to "reveal" or "unveil." The revelation comes in the form of visions and stories that use symbols and characters to explain spiritual realities. This type of writing finds its setting in a particular historical period. The meaning of the symbols is related to that period of time or to another, later period of time. An unusual feature of Daniel is that it was originally written in two different languages, with about half of the book (2:4–7:28) written in Aramaic and the rest of the book written in Hebrew. Though the setting of the book is in the period of the exile in Babylon, the events in history to which it addresses itself occur as late as the desecration of the Second Temple during Antiochus's persecution of the Jews in 167 BCE. The book of Daniel is composed of two major sections. In section one (chaps. 1–6), there are six separate, distinct tales involving Daniel and his three companions: Hananiah, Mishael, and Azaiah. The four were given Babylonian names—Belteshazzar, Shadrach, Meshach, and Abednego, respectively. God blesses Daniel and his friends with the ability to know and interpret the dreams of the king. There are the very familiar tales of the fiery furnace and lion's den plus other stories that show the four young men's unswerving faith in God, the one true, holy God of Israel. These stories are told as if by one who observed the events.

Section two of the book is a series of visions that are presented in the first person by Daniel. The visions tell of the rise and fall of kings and nations over a period of many years. Both the tales in section one and the visions in section two underscore the foundational truth the book intends to present: the Lord God Almighty is the only true God, creator of all there is, and the only ruler worthy of one's service and worship. This God blesses those who are steadfast in their faithfulness and devotion to God and brings the downfall of those who do not worship and serve God. The book of Daniel was written to provide comfort, encouragement, and hope for those faithful Jews who were suffering under the persecution of cruel, self-serving rulers. The book ends with a promise of eternal life for the righteous.

Psalms to Pray When You Experience Times of . . .

. . . Defeat and Depression
Psalm 25: "I look to the LORD for help at all times."
Psalm 27: "Trust in the LORD. Have faith, do not despair."

. . . Joy and Celebration
Psalm 95: "Come, let us praise the LORD!"
Psalm 146: "I will sing to my God all my life."

. . . Suffering and Grief
Psalm 6: "I am worn out with grief."
Psalm 30: "You have changed my sadness into a joyful dance."

. . . Seeking God's Presence in Your Life
Psalm 63: "My soul is thirsty for you."
Psalm 139:1–17: "LORD, you have examined me and you know me."

. . . Need for Guidance and Direction
Psalm 16: "My future is in your hands."
Psalm 86:1–13b: "Teach me, LORD, what you want me to do."

. . . Need for Forgiveness of Sin
Psalm 32: "Blessed are those whose sins are forgiven."
Psalm 51: "Create in me a clean heart, O God."

. . . Need for Comfort
Psalm 23: "The LORD is my shepherd."
Psalm 71: "Don't stay so far away, O God; my God, hurry to my aid."

All of the above quotes are from the TEV. This translation is recommended for these topics because the psalms are expressed in a more personalized style that lends itself to praying, as if they were our own prayers.

As you read a psalm, select one or two verses that focus your own thoughts and feelings. After you select the verse or two, read it/them several times. Then close your eyes and repeat the words slowly and prayerfully. Repeat the words at least ten times.

Something else you can do to allow these psalms to prompt your prayers is to write down on a blank sheet of paper the words of the one or two verses you selected. After you write the words down, continue writing for another five to ten minutes. Write whatever comes to mind. Write the words as your prayer to God.

Part 2

LEADER'S GUIDE

Guidelines for Bible Study Leaders

The Course's Origin

This course was first presented as part of the adult education program of the First Presbyterian Church in Livermore, California. At the time, I was a Parish Associate for the church. Pat Griggs was chair of the Adult Education and Nurture Committee. She said to me one day, "We need a Bible study course for those folks who think everyone else in the church knows more about the Bible than they do. We need a course that will provide a helpful overview of the whole Bible and will introduce the class members to basic tools and skills for Bible study, and at the same time be fun and interesting. We want you to teach that course." Well, one doesn't decline an invitation like that, especially when the chair of the committee is one's wife. The original course was for fourteen sessions and covered the Old Testament and the New Testament. The course in this book features only the Old Testament. A second volume, *The Bible from Scratch: The New Testament for Beginners,* is also available from Westminster John Knox Press.

Goals of the Course

As I planned this course, I had several goals in mind for the group members. I expected that the participants would:

1. become more comfortable using the Bible by being able to find books, chapters, and verses more easily;
2. gain a sense of the general "sweep" of the biblical story: to identify familiar persons and events, to see their connection with one another, and to get a sense of chronology;
3. be introduced to basic Bible study tools such as concordance, Bible dictionary, atlas, and commentary;
4. appreciate the value of having a variety of translations, to recognize the differences between some of the translations, and to read a translation other than the one they use most of the time;
5. enjoy studying the Bible with others;
6. develop the habit of reading the Bible regularly.

These goals were achieved by many of the participants, especially those who were present for all the sessions. Hardly a week went by without one or more of the participants expressing delight in what they discovered that week. About ten of the class members did commit to further intensive study. One of the members informed me (several years later) that he was teaching a senior high Bible study class and was using his notes from this course as a basis for his planning and teaching.

Basic Teaching Principles

As I prepared the course, I was very intentional about implementing a number of basic principles for effective teaching and leading. The foundational principle was to attempt to involve everyone in every part of every session every week. That's a big goal! It was not possible to succeed with everyone every week. You will see this principle present in all of the session plans that follow. I had at least a dozen other principles in mind as I designed the course:

1. The leader serves best as companion and guide through the course.

2. The leader provides sufficient information, but not so much that the joy of discovery by the participants is lost.
3. Motivation for learning involves enjoying and completing tasks, and making choices.
4. It is often better to use selected portions of a resource rather than the complete resource.
5. Participants learn best when a variety of activities and resources are used in order to respond to their different interests, needs, and learning styles.
6. Participants need to be invited to express their feelings, ideas, and beliefs in creative ways that are appropriate to them and to the subject matter.
7. Everyone needs opportunities to share what they understand and believe.
8. Open-ended questions invite interpretation, reflection, and application.
9. Persons are nurtured in faith when they share their faith stories with one another.
10. All teaching and learning happens in planned and unplanned ways and is for the purpose of increasing biblical literacy and faithful discipleship.
11. The Bible becomes the living word of God when teachers and learners see their own faith stories expressed in Scripture.
12. The Bible provides many resources to prompt our praying, our confessing of faith, and our commitment to ministry.

Room Arrangement

Arrange the room where you meet in such a way that participants are seated at tables. Tables are very important in that they provide space for all of the materials and, just as important, the coffee cups. Tables also suggest that we are going to work; we are not here to just sit and listen to a lecture.

Everyone needs a name tag. Set up a table with hot water and makings for coffee, tea, and hot chocolate just inside the door so everyone can get a cup and then find a seat. If you have a small group, arrange the tables in a rectangle or square so that everyone can see all the other members of the group. With a small group, you will be able to be seated with them. On the other hand, if you have a large group, arrange the tables in a fan shape pointed toward the front so the participants can see the leader standing at the front of the group with a white board and/or newsprint easel.

Resources

For the first session, be sure to provide Bibles for those who do not bring one. Continue to provide Bibles for those occasions when it is important for everyone to have the same translation and edition so that you can all look at the same pages at the same time. However, continue to encourage everyone to bring his or her own Bible. In addition to the Bibles, borrow from the church library, the pastor's library, and your own library, as many copies of concise concordances, Bible dictionaries, and Bible atlases as you can find. It is important to put these resources in the hands of the group members so they can actually practice using the tools for Bible study. You will be surprised to see how many persons buy new Bibles, dictionaries, and other resources after they are exposed to them during the course.

A church library will not ordinarily have enough Bible dictionaries for each person to have one with which to work. For those sessions where members are responsible for searching for information about a Bible person or event, make photocopies of the appropriate articles in a Bible dictionary, encyclopedia, or atlas. For one-time use, for one class, this is not a violation of copyright laws.

Be sure to provide paper and pencils for those who don't bring them. Almost all of the activity sheets to be used by the participants are at the end of the respective session plans for which they will be used. There are several other activity sheets that will need to be reproduced for the participants.

Time

I have planned each session to be an hour in length. If you have less than an hour, you will have to make some adjustments. It will be better to leave an activity out than to rush class members through all of the planned activities. Perhaps it is possible in your situation to schedule more than seven sessions. There is probably enough material here for ten sessions. If you have that much time, you will truly be able to deal with everything carefully, without hurrying.

A Final Word

As you prepare to teach this course, it is essential that you read each chapter of part 1 as you consider your teaching strategy for each session of the course. You should assume that many, though not all, of the participants will have read the respective chapter before coming to the class session, and you should be as familiar with the material as they are. Exploring the Bible with fellow pilgrims on the journey of faith will be for them and for you, the leader, a challenging, inspiring, growing, and satisfying experience. May God bless you with many discoveries and much joy on this journey. If you and the members of your Bible study group have found this course to be helpful, you may want to plan for a second course on the New Testament based on *The Bible from Scratch: The New Testament for Beginners*.

Session 1
Introducing the Bible

BEFORE THE SESSION
Focus of the Session

In this first session, it will be important to take time for participants to become comfortable with the room, with one another, and with you as the leader. It will also be a time of getting acquainted with some of the basics of reading and studying the Bible, such as using the table of contents, locating specific passages, reviewing abbreviations for Bible books, and sharing results of the Bible Skills and Tools Inventory. In addition, there will be an opening prayer activity and time to explore several New Testament passages that speak of "the scriptures."

Advanced Preparation

- Read all of the passages suggested in the material for the participants.

- Read the introductory articles in a study Bible.
- Read articles in a Bible dictionary that deal with Scripture, translation, oral tradition, canon, and language.

Physical Arrangements

Reread the section of the introduction that offers suggestions regarding room arrangement, resources and materials, and refreshments. It is important to have everything ready and in order for the first session. First impressions are very important, especially for those who are new to Bible study.

DURING THE SESSION

Welcome of Participants

Arrive at class early enough to set up the refreshments and to have everything ready before the first person arrives. Ask the participants to sign in and make name tags for themselves. Greet each one by name and with a warm welcome. If you have a display of books and resources, invite participants to spend time browsing before the session begins. As the group gathers, be sure to remind them of the four suggestions on page 4. Check to see who needs to borrow a Bible and give them one. Encourage these persons to bring Bibles next week.

Opening Prayer

On page 3 begins Psalm 92:1–4. Invite the participants to pray the words in unison, or to alternate lines between men and women or between one-half of the group and the other half. After the prayer, ask those who are willing to share some of the things they wrote in their books as they reflected on the passage during the week.

Getting Acquainted

Invite the participants to introduce themselves by sharing their names and an early memory associated with the Bible. Some will have memories from childhood, while others may have memories of more recent experiences. This is not a time for long stories, just brief vignettes. If you have a large group, you may want to form smaller groups for this exercise. Remind the participants they can get up to refill their beverage cup at any time and that you are open to any questions they may have at any time.

Bible Basics

Ask everyone to turn in their Bibles to the table of contents and the introductory pages following. People will have different translations. Affirm whatever translation they are using and that they will be able to learn more because of the variety that is available. You could do several things with them. Depending on the amount of time you have, you may want to be selective with the following suggestions:

- Ask participants to share some of the "things I notice."
- Practice pronouncing some of the more difficult names of Bible books.
- Spend a few minutes responding to some of the "questions I have."
- Participants have looked at book abbreviations in their Bibles and in chapter 1. Spend a few minutes practicing identifying books by their abbreviations. Start with a few that are fairly obvious and then use some examples that may be a little more difficult.

Next, ask everyone to turn to the first page of the book of Genesis. Ask how many have Bibles with introductions to each book. This may be a good time to make a pitch for purchasing a study Bible. Make your own recommendations or direct them to the appendix. There are several brief activities you can do with the first pages of Genesis.

- Invite participants to share "things I notice."
- Review the skill of reading Bible citations by book, chapter, and verses by writing down some examples and asking for confirmation of what is designated. Be sure to use abbreviations to identify the Bible books.
- Ask persons to share any of their list of "questions I have." Don't spend a lot of time on this. If there are a lot of questions, write them down on a sheet of newsprint with the heading "loose ends." Keep this list in front of the class week to week, and be sure to respond to all of the questions before the last session of the class.

The Scriptures

Turn to the worksheet, "The Scriptures," found on page 84. The directions are clear on the worksheet, but review them to be sure everyone knows what is expected. Check to see if all of the passages have been selected. If not, ask if there are any pairs who would be willing to work on their second choice among those that have not been selected. Encourage the class members to work in pairs. One direction to emphasize is that after each in the pair has read the passage, they are to begin discussing the three questions immediately instead of writing and then sharing their answers.

After the pairs have spent about ten minutes on the passage, ask participants to leave their partners and team up with another person or two for another ten minutes to compare notes regarding their respective passages.

Save the last task of completing the sentence for the end of the session.

Bible Skills and Tools Inventory

If everyone received their books a week or so before the class began, they may have completed the Bible Skills and Tools Inventory found on page 9. If that is not the case, you may need to provide about five minutes for them to complete it now. Afterward, ask for a show of hands on each item and have someone take notes regarding the numbers and the comments in their responses. This will be useful information for you. As you ask for responses, assure the participants that they should not feel embarrassed or proud of their answers, but that it can be helpful to know that there are others who have had as much or as little experience in studying the Bible as they have. The purpose of the course is to increase everyone's familiarity with the Bible and their confidence in using the Bible and other Bible study tools.

Closing

Ask the participants to take thirty seconds to complete the sentence that begins, "The Scriptures are . . ." After they have created their sentences, you have the ingredients of a litany. Invite everyone to share their sentences. After each has shared, the whole group will respond in unison, "O God, help us to learn and love your Holy Word." It would be good to write this unison response on a sheet of newsprint or on a chalkboard so they will know what to say.

The Scriptures

1. Work in pairs. Each pair should work on *one* of the following passages:

Matthew 4:1–11	"But [Jesus] answered, 'It is written . . ."
Luke 4:16–21	Jesus stands up to read the Scriptures.
Luke 24:13–35	Jesus explains to his companions the Scriptures.
Acts 8:26–38	"The passage of the scripture that he was reading . . ."
Acts 17:1–15	"[They] examined the scriptures every day . . ."
Romans 15:1–13	"By the encouragement of the scriptures . . ."
2 Timothy 3:10–17	"All scripture is inspired by God."

2. After reading the passage, reflect on three questions:

   What is the specific Scripture reference or content, if any?

   What seems to be the purpose or use of the Scriptures in this passage?

   What appear to be the results from speaking, hearing, or reading the Scriptures?

Complete the following sentence:

The Scriptures are ____

Session 2
The Books of the Law

BEFORE THE SESSION

Focus of the Session

In this session you will be dealing with the books of the Pentateuch, the first five books of the Hebrew Scriptures. The concept of law will be a primary focus. You will review some of the key features of each of the five books, and you will introduce and practice using Bible concordances.

Advanced Preparation

- Read the passages suggested in the material for the participants.
- Read introductory articles for each of the first five books of the Bible.

- Read articles in a Bible dictionary that deal with law, Pentateuch, acrostic psalms, and torah.
- Bring to class at least one copy each of a concordance in a study Bible, a concise concordance, and a comprehensive, or complete, concordance.
- Gather several additional translations of the Bible. It would be especially helpful if you can obtain a copy of the Tanakh, a standard Jewish Bible in English.
- Gather as many concise concordances as you are able. If you don't have enough so that each pair of persons can share a copy, then it will be important to cut and paste and copy excerpts from a concise concordance. You will find additional directions in the session plan.

DURING THE SESSION

Welcome of Participants

There will likely be persons coming to this session who were not at the first session. Be sure they are welcomed and briefed regarding what to expect. Greet all of the participants and encourage them to browse among the various translations of the Bible you have displayed on a table.

Opening Prayer

The opening prayer is in a format similar to that in session 1. Ask everyone to turn to page 12 in their books, where they will find selected verses from Psalm 119. They have already read/prayed these words and have spent some time reflecting on their meaning. Lead the prayer antiphonally, with half of the group reading one set of verses and the other half reading the indented set. If you divided the group between men and women last week, do it differently this week. After the prayer, invite the members of the group to offer any insights they care to share in response to the questions in their books.

Exploring Psalm 119

Those who read chapter 2 will have the necessary background for understanding some of the key features of Psalm 119. However, there will likely be some who did not read the material; in any case, it will be helpful to review this information for everyone. There may be some questions that folks would like to ask to reinforce or clarify their understanding. The important things to review and explore are:

- Psalm 119 is an acrostic poem or psalm. Review what an acrostic poem is. If you can make a photocopy and/or a transparency of a page of Psalm 119 from the Hebrew text, the nature of an acrostic will be very clear even if no one can read the Hebrew. Some English Bibles include the appropriate Hebrew letters at the beginning of each stanza of the psalm.
- Remind participants that in Hebrew there are twenty-two consonants in the alphabet and eight verses in each stanza of the psalm. Thus, the length of the psalm is 176 verses.
- Look at the first eight verses, the first stanza. Skim through the verses, calling attention to the synonym for *law* in each verse. If there are several different translations, so much the better. Make a list on newsprint, transparency, or chalkboard of each different word that is found.
- Assign each member of the group a different stanza of eight verses. Each member is to find the synonyms for *law* in the verses of his or her stanza. After a minute or two, invite participants to call out all of the additional words they have found. Add these to the list.
- After the list of synonyms is created, ask several questions to guide some reflection on what has been found. What does this suggest to you regarding the concept of law for the Hebrews? How is that different from what we usually think of regarding law and laws? How important is the biblical concept of law for Christians?
- Explain that Protestant Christians regard the Bible in a similar way as the Jews regard the law.
- If you have time, you could do one more activity. Direct the participants to return to the stanzas they each explored previously and to identify what type of writing or prayer it is. Is it praise, lament, thanksgiving, petition,

admonition, trust, or something else? Often a stanza will be a mixture of types. This is another interesting feature of Psalm 119.

The Five Books of the Law

You need to be careful not to get carried away with trying to cover too much material in this part of the session. What you want to accomplish is a quick review of key features of each of the five books of the Law. If you have a class of fifteen to twenty members, or fewer, divide it into five small groups. Each group is to work with a different one of the five books. If you have a larger group, assign two or more small groups the same book.

Duplicate ahead of time a brief introduction to each book from a study Bible and/or a brief article from a Bible dictionary. Some members may have Bibles with this information. Be sure each person has something to read in order to answer these questions: (1) What does the title of the book mean? (2) What is the primary theme, storyline, or content of the book? (3) What are two or three verses in the book that are worth remembering? Give the groups no more than ten minutes to do this work, and then invite each group to share its findings in the order these books appear in the Bible.

Practicing with a Bible Concordance

The participants were introduced to the nature of a concordance in chapter 2, but they haven't experienced using one unless they already have a concordance at home. It is ideal if you are able to secure a sufficient number of small or concise concordances so that each pair of persons has access to one. If that is not possible, then be sure to have examples of several types of concordances available to show their differences. If you don't have enough concordances for the participants to use, then it will be necessary to duplicate pages of a concise concordance that include the words for the following activities.

1. Ask the participants if they have heard of the passage where Jesus is asked, "Which commandment in the law is the greatest?"(Matt. 22:36). Several hands will surely be raised. Ask them, "How did Jesus answer the question?" Spend a minute recalling that his answer is known as the Great Commandment: "You shall love the Lord your God with all your heart, and with all your soul, and with all your mind" (22:37). Then ask, "Does anyone know where to find the passage?" If any

know, ask them to find it but not tell anyone. Ask the others, "Where would you start looking to find the passage?"

2. Instruct the participants who have not already done so to take a few minutes to try to find this passage. Allow just a minute or two. The participants will undoubtedly be frustrated, which will prepare them to be ready to learn about a tool that will help them find passages they know but don't know where to find them. Tell the participants that they are limited in their ability to find Bible passages by: (1) what they remember, (2) what they find by chance in their skimming, and (3) what they are directed to find by the leader.

3. Tell them there is a special book/resource/tool that is designed to help them find familiar passages as well as other passages on a particular topic. That book is a concordance. Show and explain the differences and similarities between concise and comprehensive concordances. As you are doing this, have them look at page 18, which shows brief examples of each. Check to see if anyone has a simple concordance in the back of his or her Bible.

4. Take time to practice with the concordance. Make a list of key words in the passage referred to above: *law, greatest, commandment, love, soul, heart,* and *mind.* Now, using the concordances or the handouts you prepared, have them find the passage. No doubt they will be led by one or more of the key words to Matthew 22:34–40, Mark 12:28–31, or Luke 10:25–28. When they have found all three passages, spend a few minutes calling attention to the similarities and differences of the three passages.

5. Comment that the words of Jesus' answer in Matthew and Luke are not original to him; he is quoting from the books of the Law. This provides an opportunity to introduce the value of cross-reference notes to find the source of quotes in one book of the Bible from another. Check to see if anyone in the group has a Bible with cross-reference notes. Study Bibles are especially helpful in this matter. If not, use the same key words above to find the original passages in Deuteronomy 6:5 and Leviticus 19:18.

6. If there is any time remaining, and if you have a sufficient number of concordances, you could practice finding other

familiar passages that members of the group remember but have no idea where to find.

Closing

Before the closing prayer, invite the group to share some of their answers to the questions on page 17.

Turn to page 12, where several verses of Psalm 119 are printed. Invite the participants to skim the verses to select one verse that speaks with special meaning today. After a minute, ask them to share their verses as a closing prayer. Remind them that it is okay for verses to be repeated.

Session 3

The Narratives of Genesis

BEFORE THE SESSION

Focus of the Session

This session focuses on the major narratives of Genesis. It is difficult to keep all the characters straight and to remember the events in chronological order. You and your group will not be able to master all the material in one hour, but you can gain an overview of the major persons and events in the narratives of Genesis. In this session you will also have the opportunity to compare the two creation narratives and to practice with footnotes that are in the biblical text.

Advanced Preparation

- Read the passages suggested in the material for the participants.
- Read an article or chapter of a Bible handbook or dictionary on Genesis.

- Be sure to complete the Search and Find Exercise (pages 26–27) so that you will have the correct answers when you do the activity in class.
- Gather Bibles from the sanctuary or classrooms that are all the same and have footnote references. This will make the practice with footnotes easier.
- Bring some books from your library, the pastor's library, or the church's library for the participants to browse through. Suggested books include: Bible atlas, Bible dictionary, Bible concordance, and others with information about the narratives of Genesis. By displaying books each week, you will be introducing the participants to some of the resources they may want to purchase for their own libraries if they are motivated to do more in-depth Bible study.

DURING THE SESSION

Welcome of Participants

If there are new participants who did not attend the first two sessions, be sure they are welcomed and briefed regarding what to expect. Greet all of the participants and encourage them to browse among the various translations of the Bible you have displayed on a table.

Opening Prayer

Remind the participants of their reading of Psalm 78:1–8 and review the nature of salvation history psalms and the connection between those psalms and the narratives of the book of Genesis. Direct them to turn to Hebrews 11. Call attention to all the appearances of the phrase "by faith" and the names of the persons following.

Lead the participants in a litany that you will find at the end of this session plan. You or a member of the group will read the passage and will pause each time the phrase "by faith" appears in the text. The participants are to respond in unison, speaking the phrase "by faith." At the end of the reading, invite the participants to offer statements out of their own experiences that are expressions of their faith. As the leader, speak the phrase "by faith" and then allow time for someone to respond. Speak the phrase again and wait for another person to respond. Repeat the process several more times or until you think everyone who cares to offer a statement has done so. Conclude with "Amen," and say, "And all of God's people say . . . ," and the group will respond with their own "Amen."

Practicing with Footnotes

Distribute Bibles that are all alike, with footnotes, so that it will be easier to do this activity. You could also check to see how many of the participants have Bibles with footnote references. If they have them, they could use both Bibles in order to notice their similarities and differences. Review the examples that begin on pages 24. Then direct the group to skim in the book of Genesis to find other examples of footnotes. Invite them to share things they find that are of interest to them and to ask any questions they have. Allow about ten minutes for this activity.

Comparing the Two Creation Narratives

It will be helpful for the participants to see clearly the differences and similarities between the two narratives of creation in Genesis 1 and 2. Direct the participants to the worksheet on page 97. Divide the group into pairs. Each pair is to work on just one of the two narratives. Be sure there are an equal number of pairs with each narrative. They are to answer the questions based only on their assigned narrative. Remind them that it is possible that one or more of the questions cannot be answered by their passage.

When the pairs have completed the task, they will team up with a pair that worked on the other passage so that they can compare their answers to see the differences and similarities. If you judge that time is limited, you could gather responses to each question from the whole group. This would work best if you had a large chart on newsprint or whiteboard or overhead transparency so that as you record the answers, everyone will be able to see them. When the chart is completed, spend a few minutes reflecting on the results of the exploration. One question to ask is, "Based on your own experience and reasoning ability, how would you account for the differences and similarities between these two narratives?"

Getting the Narratives Straight

On page 98 at the end of this session plan is a page with eighteen cards, each with a different narrative or set of narratives. You will need to copy this page and then cut the cards apart. Distribute the cards so that each person has one card. If you have a large group, participants can work in pairs. If you have fewer than eighteen, eliminate some of the cards. Each person, with his or her card, is to do three things:

1. Find the chapter(s) in Genesis where the narrative is found.
2. Notice what narratives immediately precede and follow the narrative of their search.
3. Skim the chapter(s) to find one to three verses that are meaningful, that the participant would like to share with the whole group.

They should be able to accomplish this task in about ten to fifteen minutes.

After everyone has completed the assignment, give them the following instructions. They are to stand up, talk with others to see where their narrative fits, and then arrange themselves in the chronological sequence of the narratives in Genesis. There will be a lot of scrambling, which is part of the fun of the activity. After they are in the correct sequence, invite each member to state the title of his or her narrative and to read the one to three verses that were selected. Take a few minutes to reflect on the experience of the activity to see what has been learned and to respond to any questions that arise.

A Search and Find Exercise

On pages 26–27 is a Search and Find Exercise. Some may have completed it and others will not have worked on it. You could quickly lead the whole group through the exercise so that those who have answers will be able to share them while those who didn't complete the exercise will be able to write the answers in the appropriate blanks. The purpose of this activity (and the previous one), is to help the participants become familiar with the major persons and events of the narratives of Genesis and to make some connections between the various persons. This is clearly not an in-depth study of Genesis. If some of the class members show interest in learning more, you could encourage them to recommend to the adult education planning team that a Bible study on Genesis be offered some time in the future.

Closing

Before closing the session with prayer, invite the participants to share some of their thoughts in response to the third question related to their reading and reflecting on Psalm 78:1–8 found on page 21. This could be a very rich time of sharing.

Conclude by offering a prayer of thanksgiving. Ask each person to think of one or more persons who have been instrumental in her or his faith formation and spiritual nurture, persons who have shared the good news of the mighty acts and wondrous deeds of God. Invite them, one at a time, to name a person. After each participant has named a person, the whole group will respond in unison, "Thanks be to God for this faithful witness."

By Faith

A Litany

Based on Hebrews 11:1–22

Now faith is the assurance of things hoped for, the conviction of things not seen. Indeed, **by faith** our ancestors received approval. **By faith** we understand that the worlds were prepared by the word of God, so that what is seen was made from things that are not visible.

By faith Abel offered to God a more acceptable sacrifice than Cain's. Through this he received approval as righteous, God himself giving approval to his gifts; he died, but through his faith he still speaks. **By faith** Enoch was taken so that he did not experience death; and "he was not found, because God had taken him." For it was attested before he was taken away that "he had pleased God." And without faith it is impossible to please God, for whoever would approach him must believe that he exists and that he rewards those who seek him. **By faith** Noah, warned by God about events as yet unseen, respected the warning and built an ark to save his household; by this he condemned the world and became an heir to the righteousness that is in accordance with faith.

By faith Abraham obeyed when he was called to set out for a place that he was to receive as an inheritance; and he set out, not knowing where he was going. **By faith** he stayed for a time in the land he had been promised, as in a foreign land, living in tents, as did Isaac and Jacob, who were heirs with him of the same promise. For he looked forward to the city that has foundations, whose architect and builder is God. **By faith** he received power of procreation, even though he was too old— and Sarah herself was barren— because he considered him faithful who had promised. Therefore from one person, and this one as good as dead, descendants were born, "as many as the stars of heaven and as the innumerable grains of sand by the seashore."

All of these died in faith without having received the promises, but from a distance they saw and greeted them. They confessed that they were strangers and foreigners on the earth, for people who speak in this way make it clear that they are seeking a homeland. . . . Therefore God is not ashamed to be called their God; indeed, he has prepared a city for them.

By faith Abraham, when put to the test, offered up Isaac. He who had received the promises was ready to offer up his only son, of whom he had been told, "It is through Isaac that descendants shall be named for you." . . . *By faith* Isaac invoked blessings for the future on Jacob and Esau. **By faith** Jacob, when dying, blessed each of the sons of Joseph, "bowing in worship over the top of his staff." **By faith** Joseph, at the end of his life, made mention of the exodus of the Israelites and gave instructions about his burial.

Comparing the Creation Narratives

Group 1: Genesis 1:1–2:4a		Group 2: Genesis 2:4b–25
1.	How long did creation take?	1.
2.	Where did creation take place?	2.
3.	When in the process was man created?	3.
4.	When in the process was woman created?	4.
5.	From what "substance" are man and woman created?	5.
6.	What is the relationship between male and female?	6.
7.	What is the relationship between human beings and God?	7.
8.	What is the main point or message of the narrative?	8.

Seven days of creation	Adam and Eve in the garden	Cain and Abel
Noah and the flood	The tower of Babel	Abraham and Sarah
Birth of Isaac	Isaac and Rebekah	Jacob tricks Esau
Jacob tricks Isaac	Jacob and Laban	Jacob and Leah
Jacob and Rachel	Jacob reunited with Esau	Joseph sold by his brothers
Joseph becomes governor of Egypt	Joseph's brothers go to Egypt for grain	Joseph reunited with his father, Jacob

Session 4

From Egypt to Canaan

BEFORE THE SESSION

Focus of the Session

In this session we will work on gaining an overview of the period of history from the birth of Moses to the death of Joshua. This covers a large portion of Exodus, Numbers, and Joshua. We will only be able to skim the surface and will not introduce any new Bible exploring skills or resources this session. However, there will be one major activity that will require careful preparation.

Advanced Preparation

- Read the passages suggested in the material for the participants.
- Read articles in a Bible dictionary or encyclopedia on Moses, ark of the Lord, tabernacle, manna, Red Sea, Ten Commandments, and Joshua.

- Find or prepare a timeline that shows the period of Israel's history that is featured in this session. It would be good to keep this timeline in front of the class for the rest of the course.
- If you can find a large map showing the route of the exodus, display it prominently.
- Gather material for twenty large name tags or as many as you need for the number in your class. Use half-sheets of colored construction paper, felt markers, and masking tape. The participants will use these in the major activity of the class.

DURING THE SESSION

God Calls Moses

Instead of beginning immediately with an opening prayer prompted by Scripture, explain to the group that they are going to focus first on the key character of today's session, Moses. Review with them what they read the past week and what they already know about Moses, from the time of his birth to his encounter with God at the burning bush while he was tending the flocks of his father-in-law.

Invite the members of the group to do a little brainstorming about the various roles of Moses at the time of his call by God at the burning bush. You should be able to gather from the group most of the following: shepherd, husband, son-in-law, Hebrew, Pharaoh's adopted son, Midianite, killer, fugitive, observer, protector, listener to God, called to be a leader. Write these roles on newsprint or chalkboard. When you have a list of ten or so, ask, "Which of these roles would likely influence Moses to want to stay in Midian and which would influence him to return to Egypt?" Make two lists, one under the heading "Stay in Midian" and the other under "Return to Egypt." Assign half of the group to listen to the passage you will read as if they were Moses wanting to stay in Midian, and assign the other half to listen as if they were Moses deciding to return to Egypt.

Tell the group you will read Exodus 3:1–11a and that you are going to end the reading with the line, "But Moses said to God." At this point, the members of the group are to respond in the role of Moses that they were assigned. They will be arguing among themselves as Moses might have debated within himself whether to stay in Midian or return to Egypt. After a minute or two of this, call time and then take a few more minutes to reflect on the experience. Guide the debriefing with a question or two: What did you experience as Moses? How much of a struggle do you think Moses had in deciding what to do? When have you had difficulty deciding what God wanted you to do?

Opening Prayer

Turn to page 103 for "God's Word to Moses and to Us." Before leading the litany, call attention to the last line, where the participants are asked to complete a sentence that begins, "O God" Tell them that when you have read the line that begins, "God said, 'Now, go!'" there will be a brief time of silence for them to write or think of a completion to the sentence. Lead the group in the litany. When you have read the last line, allow about thirty seconds of silence, then read the line again. After someone speaks her or his sentence, read the line again. Repeat the process until you think all who want to share have shared. You may want to conclude this opening time by singing the hymn, "Here I Am, Lord."

Introduction to the Scope of the Story in This Session

Ask the group to turn to Exodus 1:1–14. Read the passage, then call attention to the links between last week's study in Genesis and what is to come this week. Explain that the focus will be on two main characters, Moses and Joshua, with a number of supporting characters. If you have a timeline to refer to, show the period of history that will be covered in this session.

Twenty Examples of God's Mighty Acts of Deliverance

Those who read chapter 4 will have a sense of the storyline of these twenty episodes in the story of deliverance between Egypt and Canaan. However, it is unlikely that many, if anyone, will have read all the biblical references that were suggested. This activity will help each participant focus on one of the twenty episodes and gain an overview of the whole story represented by these events. The activity will take the following steps:

1. Turn to page 104 for the worksheet, "Twenty Stories between Egypt and Canaan."
2. Ask the members of the group to each select one of the stories to be her or his focus. If you have fewer than twenty in the group, do either of two things: (1) eliminate an appropriate number of stories or (2) go with whatever stories the

members select. The latter is likely the best strategy since that way everyone will have his or her own choice. If you have more than twenty participants, ask some people to work together.

3. Review the directions on the worksheet. Each person is to read his or her passage and then answer the three questions listed. Remind the participants that this is not a term paper project but to work quickly and not get bogged down in the details.
4. Allow about fifteen minutes for reading and answering the questions.
5. Ask the participants to meet in groups of three and for each person to summarize the story of his or her passage.
6. Get the whole group's attention to explain the next step in the activity. Each person is to select one of the characters in his or her story with which to identify. The character could be someone named or an imaginary person. They are to write the name of the person on a large name tag and attach it to their clothing.
7. The members of the group are now to arrange themselves in chronological order based on their story.
8. Starting with the first episode, each person is to tell her or his story in the first person in the role of the character on the name tag. Remind the group that these are to be very short stories.
9. After all have introduced themselves, conclude by asking a question: What are some impressions you have of your faith family's history? What do you think about God's role in this history?

Closing

Turn to page 105 for "We Will Serve the Lord!" As the leader, you can take the role of Joshua in the reading, and all of the members of the group will read in unison the part of the people. You will also need a volunteer to read the narrator's part.

God's Word to Moses and to Us

Leader: God said to Moses from the burning bush, "Moses, Moses." (Exodus 3:4)

People: Help us, God, to hear you when you speak to us, and to say as Moses did, "Here I am."

L. God said, "Take off your sandals, for the place where you are standing is holy ground." (Exodus 3:5)

P. Remind us, O God, that wherever you meet us, that is a holy place.

L. God said, "I have seen how cruelly my people are being treated in Egypt; I have heard them cry out to be rescued." (Exodus 3:7)

P. May we see through your eyes, the needs of people to be rescued and may we be willing to respond to their cry.

L. God said, "I am sending you so that you can lead my people." (Exodus 3:10)

P. We are overwhelmed by the immensity of the task that you place before us; give us strength and wisdom, O God, sufficient for the task.

L. God said, "I AM WHO I AM. This is my name forever; this is what all future generations will call me." (Exodus 3:14,15)

P. Thank you, God, for revealing to us your name and yourself, so that we may know you as the One who delivers all who call upon you.

L. God said, "Now, go! I will help you speak and will teach you what to say." (Exodus 4:12)

P. [Write your own sentence prayer response to God.]

O God, . . .

Twenty Stories between Egypt and Canaan

A. Each member of the class will work on *one* of the following passages/events.

1. Moses' birth and early years	Exod. 2:1–25
2. Moses called by God to return to Egypt	Exod. 3:1–4:31
3. Moses' and Aaron's first efforts to free the slaves	Exod. 5:1–6:12
4. The nine plagues on the Egyptians	Exod. 7:12–11:10
5. The passover	Exod. 12:1–29
6. The exodus	Exod. 12:29–42 and 13:17–14:4
7. The crossing of the sea	Exod. 14:5–31 and 15:19–21
8. Manna and quail	Exod. 16:1–35
9. At Mount Sinai	Exod. 19:1–20:21
10. The ark of the Lord and the tabernacle	Exod. 25:1–26:37
11. The golden calf	Exod. 32:1–33:3
12. Second set of Ten Commandments	Exod. 33:12–34:35
13. Complaints in the wilderness	Num. 11:1–34
14. Spies sent to explore Canaan	Num. 13:1–3, 16–33
15. The people rebel against God and Moses	Num. 14:1–45
16. Renewal of the covenant	Deut. 29:1–18 and 30:11–20
17. Joshua succeeds Moses and the death of Moses	Deut. 31:1–29 and 34:1–12
18. The crossing of the Jordan	Josh. 1:1–18 and 3:1–4:24
19. The fall of Jericho	Josh. 5:13–6:27
20. Joshua leads people to renew covenant	Josh. 24:1–28

B. Each individual will read his/her passage and answer the following questions.

1. What is God's action in this passage? For what purpose?
2. What is the response of the people to God's action?
3. What are the consequences of the people's response?

We Will Serve the Lord!

(Based on Joshua 24:14–27, NIV)

Joshua: Now fear the LORD and serve him with all faithfulness. Throw away the gods your ancestors worshiped beyond the River and in Egypt, and serve the LORD. But if serving the LORD seems undesirable to you, then choose for yourselves this day whom you will serve, whether the gods your ancestors served beyond the River, or the gods of the Amorites, in whose land you are living. But as for me and my household, we will serve the LORD.

People: Far be it from us to forsake the LORD to serve other gods! It was the LORD our God himself who brought us and our ancestors up out of Egypt, from that land of slavery, and performed those great signs before our eyes. He protected us on our entire journey and among all the nations through which we traveled. And the LORD drove out before us all the nations, including the Amorites, who lived in the land. We too will serve the LORD, because he is our God.

Joshua: You are not able to serve the LORD. He is a holy God; he is a jealous God. He will not forgive your rebellion and your sins. If you forsake the Lord and serve foreign gods, he will turn and bring disaster on you and make an end of you, after he has been good to you.

People: No! We will serve the LORD.

Joshua: You are witnesses against yourselves that you have chosen to serve the LORD.

People: Yes, we are witnesses.

Joshua: Now then, throw away the foreign gods that are among you and yield your hearts to the LORD, the God of Israel.

People: We will serve the LORD our God and obey him.

Narrator: On that day Joshua made a covenant for the people, and there at Shechem he drew up for them decrees and laws. And Joshua recorded these things in the Book of the Law of God. Then he took a large stone and set it up there under the oak near the holy place of the LORD.

Joshua: See! This stone will be a witness against us. It has heard all the words the LORD has said to us. It will be a witness against you if you are untrue to your God.

People: We will serve the LORD our God and obey him.

Session 5
From Joshua to Nehemiah

BEFORE THE SESSION

Focus of the Session

We have a big task ahead of us in this session as we move through about eight hundred years of history, from the conquest of Canaan led by Joshua to the resettlement of Jerusalem by the exiles after their return from Babylon. There will be a couple of brief activities and one major activity for the session. The goals we will seek to accomplish are: (1) Make a connection between the books of the Law and the books of history; (2) gain a sense of the general timeline between Joshua and Nehemiah; (3) identify key persons and events in the eight-hundred-year span of history; (4) become acquainted with one of the nineteen characters of the study; and (5) relate the key persons and events to the importance of the covenant between God and the people.

Advanced Preparation

- Read the passages in the material suggested for the participants.
- Read articles in a Bible dictionary or encyclopedia on the three collections in the Hebrew Scriptures (Law, Prophets, and Writings), Jerusalem, Temple, Deuteronomic History, priest, exile, and Babylonia.
- Duplicate page 112 as a handout for the participants. Before the session, print the names of the persons, one on each handout. There are nineteen Bible characters in this session's study. If you have fewer than nineteen in your group, select which you think will be the most representative characters. If you have more, assign two group members to particular characters or add some others whom you think would be worth studying.
- Gather sufficient resources for the participants to use in their research for the major exploration activity. In addition to the material in chapter 5, the participants need at least one article from a Bible dictionary, encyclopedia, or "people of the Bible" book about their Bible character. If you don't have enough books, one way to provide these articles is to photocopy the relevant articles and give each person one or two related to his or her character.
- Create a long timeline on one of the walls of the room. (If necessary, extend the timeline around the corner onto two walls.) Create the timeline using a roll of adding machine paper marked off in fifty-year segments of about eighteen to twenty-four inches each, beginning with 1300 BCE and ending at 500 BCE. You will need a roll of masking tape for the participants to attach their information sheets to the timeline at the end of the activity.

DURING THE SESSION

Opening Prayer

The participants were introduced to the psalm type, *salvation history psalms,* also referred to as *psalms of the mighty acts of God,* in chapter 3. In this session, which covers a period of eight hundred years, we read of many of God's mighty acts for the salvation, or deliverance, of the people of Israel. One of the five psalms of this type, Psalm 136, is presented in the form of a litany. The first half of each verse recalls a mighty act of God, with the second half of the verse repeating the line, "for his steadfast love endures forever." Each of the five salvation history psalms features a different sequence of events in the history of the people of Israel. Psalm 106:40–48 presents the period of time covered in this session. On page 111 you will find a litany that blends the mighty acts of God from Psalm 106 with the litany response of Psalm 136.

Before leading the group in this litany, remind the group of the nature of salvation history psalms and explain the composition of the litany as described above. If you are familiar with the Hebrew word *hesed,* translated as "steadfast love," you could share a little about the word's meaning. Ask the group members to take turns reading the "leader" sections, with the whole group responding in unison with "God's steadfast love endures forever." At the conclusion of the litany, invite participants to add their own brief statements that express how God has acted in their lives. After each has shared, the group will continue with the unison response as in the litany.

The Books of History and Law and the Timeline

Ask the group to turn to the table of contents in their Bibles. Identify the books of the Pentateuch that were the focus of last week's study. Call the group's attention to the books that follow from Joshua through Nehemiah. Speak about the nature of this section, which is often referred to as books of history but is included in the Hebrew Scriptures' collection known as the Prophets. Ezra, Nehemiah, and the two books of Chronicles are the exceptions, as they are included in the collection of The Writings. Say a few words about the nature of 1 and 2 Chronicles. Speak about Joshua being the "bridge person" between last week's study and this week's. Finally, call attention to the timelines on page 49 and on the wall.

Exploring Key Characters and Events from Joshua to Nehemiah

This is the major activity of the session, which you should be able to complete in thirty to forty minutes. Following is the sequence of the activity, with a few suggestions on how to lead it successfully.

1. Introduce the activity by explaining what the group will be doing in the next half hour or so.

2. Distribute the worksheets you prepared ahead of time, one for each member of the group, each with a different name of one of the Bible characters in this week's study and its related Bible passages. You can ask either for volunteers to take the worksheets in turn, or you can just hand them out randomly.

3. Explain several things: (a) Participants are not preparing a term paper but just gathering some basic information about their Bible character, so they should work quickly. (b) They are to use the article(s) you have prepared, the suggested Bible passages, and chapter 5 of this book in order to find the answers to the questions on the worksheet. (c) They will attach their worksheets to the timeline mounted on the wall of the room at the place closest to the date relevant to their Bible character.

4. While the members of the group are working independently, circulate among them in order to provide assistance. If you see some are having difficulty finding information, give some suggestions on where to look or ask some probing questions to guide them to the answers.

5. After everyone has attached a worksheet to the timeline, you can take one of two approaches, depending on how much time remains in the session. One approach would be for the group to stand in front of the timeline and for you to comment on each of the Bible characters and to make any special points that will help tie one character to another. The other approach would be to ask each member of the group to speak, briefly summarizing his or her Bible character. The second approach is better but likely will take a little longer.

6. The last step of the activity is to engage the group in a time of reflection and discussion about this period of history in the life of God's people. It would be best to stay close to the timeline. Some possible questions are:
   - What underlying theme or thread do you see tying together the persons and events of these eight hundred years?
   - What word or phrase would you use to summarize this period of history?
   - What is one key question you have about this time period?

- What connections do you see between the persons and events in this period and what is happening in the world, the church, and/or your life today?

Closing

There are several possibilities for closing the session. You could do all or one of the following, depending on how much time is left in the session: (1) Close with a prayer offered by yourself or a member of the group. (2) Sing a hymn such as "For All the Saints" and offer a prayer. (3) Read a passage from a book of the Apocrypha, The Wisdom of Jesus Son of Sirach, also known as Ecclesiasticus. This book was compiled around 180 BCE and was used for teaching the faithful. If you are able to find some additional information about this book, you could share a few highlights before reading the passage. The passage captures very well the theme of these eight hundred years of history that involved so many leaders of God's chosen people. You will find the passage on page 113.

The Steadfast Love of the Lord Endures Forever

(Based upon Psalm 106:40–48)

Leader: Then the anger of the LORD was kindled against his people, and he abhorred his heritage.

Group: *God's steadfast love endures forever.*

Leader: He gave them into the hand of the nations, so that those who hated them ruled over them.

Group: *God's steadfast love endures forever.*

Leader: Their enemies oppressed them, and they were brought into subjection under their power.

Group: *God's steadfast love endures forever.*

Leader: Many times he delivered them, but they were rebellious in their purposes, and were brought low through their iniquity.

Group: *God's steadfast love endures forever.*

Leader: Nevertheless he regarded their distress when he heard their cry.

Group: *God's steadfast love endures forever.*

Leader: For their sake he remembered his covenant, and showed compassion according to the abundance of his steadfast love.

Group: *God's steadfast love endures forever.*

Leader: He caused them to be pitied by all who held them captive.

Group: *God's steadfast love endures forever.*

Leader: Save us, O LORD our God, and gather us from among the nations, that we may give thanks to your holy name and glory in your praise.

Group: *God's steadfast love endures forever.*

Leader: Blessed be the LORD, the God of Israel, from everlasting to everlasting. And let all the people say, "Amen." Praise the LORD!

Group: *God's steadfast love endures forever.*

Exploring a Key Bible Character

Name

Approximate Date

Person's Role or Position

Person's Key Relationships

Major Events Involving the Person

God's Place in the Story

Key Characters and Events from Joshua to Nehemiah

Person	Bible Passages
Joshua	Josh. 1:1–9; 14:1–15; and 24:14–28
Gideon	Judg. 6:1–24 and 7:1–22
Hannah	1 Sam. 1:1–27 and 2:18–26
Samuel (boy)	1 Sam. 2:11–26 and 3:1–4:1
Samuel (man)	1 Sam. 7:15–8:22 and 10:17–27
Saul	1 Sam. 10:1–27; 14:47–15:35
David (boy)	1 Sam. 16:1–23; 17:12–27, 38–51
David (in hiding)	1 Sam. 18:6–16; 19:11–18; 22:1–5; and 23:1–14
Jonathan	1 Sam. 20:1–42
David (king)	2 Sam. 5:1–5; 6:1–23; and 11:1–27
Nathan	2 Sam. 7:1–17; 12:1–25; and 1 Kgs. 1:38–40
Solomon	1 Kgs. 2:1–4; 3:1–15; 4:20, 21, 29–34; 6:1–14; and 11:9–13
Rehoboam	1 Kgs. 11:9–13; 11:41–12:19; and 14:21–31
Jeroboam	1 Kgs. 11:26–40 and 12:20, 25–13:34
Elijah	1 Kgs. 18:1–19:21
Hezekiah	2 Kgs. 18:1–8; 19:1–19, 32–36; and 20:1–21
Josiah	2 Kgs. 22:1–23:25
Ezra	Ezra 1:1–7; 7:1–10, 27–28; 8:21–23; and Neh. 8:1–12
Nehemiah	Neh. 1:1–2:8; 5:14–19; and 7:73b–8:18

Hymn in Honor of Our Ancestors

Sirach 44:1–15

Let us now sing the praises of famous men [and women],
our ancestors in their generations.
The Lord apportioned to them great glory,
his majesty from the beginning.
There were those who ruled in their kingdoms,
and made a name for themselves by their valor;
those who gave counsel because they were intelligent;
those who spoke in prophetic oracles;
those who led the people by their counsels
and by their knowledge of the people's lore;
they were wise in their words of instruction;
those who composed musical tunes,
or put verses in writing;
rich men endowed with resources
living peacefully in their homes—
all these were honored in their generations
and were the pride of their times.
Some of them have left behind a name,
so that others declare their praise.
But of others there is no memory;
they have perished as though they had never existed;
they have become as though they had never been born,
they and their children after them.
But these also were godly men,
whose righteous deeds have not been forgotten;
their wealth will remain with their descendants,
and their inheritance with their children's children.
Their descendants stand by the covenants;
their children also, for their sake.
Their offspring will continue forever,
and their glory will never be blotted out.
Their bodies are buried in peace,
but their name lives on generation after generation.
The assembly declares their wisdom,
and the congregation proclaims their praise.

Session 6
The Books of the Prophets

BEFORE THE SESSION

Focus of the Session

There are fifteen books of the Prophets in the Old Testament.[1] In this session we will focus on seven: Isaiah, Jeremiah, Ezekiel, Hosea, Amos, Jonah, and Micah. The material for the participants in chapter 6 presents some basic information about each of the books as well as the prophets themselves. You will want to supplement that material with what you have gathered from your own study and experience with those seven prophets. In this session you will want to (1) make connections between the prophets and the settings in which they prophesied; (2) help the participants see the themes of judgment and the call for justice and righteousness that pervade all of the prophets; (3) guide each participant to focus on one prophet for further exploration; and, (4) relate the messages of the prophets

1. See the introduction to chapter 6, which describes the differences between the collection in the Hebrew Scriptures known as the Prophets and the books Christians commonly refer to as prophetic.

to the life of faith in God today. If you do not have a full hour for the session, you should consider omitting the activity, "God Calls Isaiah, Jeremiah, and Jonah."

Advanced Preparation

- Read the passages in the material suggested for the participants.
- Read articles in a Bible dictionary or encyclopedia on these key words: *prophet, prophecy, judgment, righteousness, remnant,* and *messianic hope*.
- Duplicate page 121 as a handout for the participants. Before the session, print the names of the prophets on the handouts. There are seven prophets. If you have fourteen or more participants, you will have at least seven small groups of two to four persons each. If you have fewer than fourteen, omit one or two of the prophets. Prepare as many handouts for each prophet as there will be persons in the small groups.
- Gather sufficient resources for the participants to use in their research for the major exploration activity. In addition to the material in chapter 6, each participant needs at least one article from a Bible dictionary or an introductory article from a study Bible about his or her prophet. One way to provide these articles if you don't have enough books is to photocopy the relevant articles.
- You will want to use the long timeline again. If it was removed after the last session, attach it again to the wall.

DURING THE SESSION

Opening Prayer

The opening prayer for this session is both a dramatic reading and a prayer from the prophet Jeremiah (see pages 118–119). Set the stage by referring to Jeremiah's call to be a prophet, to the words he was given by God to proclaim to the people, and to his despair at the people's response to his message from the Lord. Since you want the participants to identify with Jeremiah, they will read his words in unison. The other character in the drama is the Lord. A dramatic way to read this part is to have someone with a very commanding voice read the words using a microphone and speaker. It would be good if that person could be hidden and even more dramatic if there is a way to alter the sound so that the words of the Lord appear to be coming from a distant, holy place. When all is ready, proceed with the reading. After the reading, ask the participants to reflect on Jeremiah's words and the experience of being Jeremiah. Ask them, "What connections would you make between these words and experiences of Jeremiah to our faith and life situation today?"

God Calls Isaiah, Jeremiah, and Jonah

In the books of Isaiah, Jeremiah, and Jonah, there are brief narratives that portray the call to each to speak the word of the Lord. These call narratives, like those of Abraham, Moses, and Gideon, follow a similar pattern, with four distinct movements or stages of the call: (1) God's call is *revealed* to the prophet. (2) The prophet *resists* the call. (3) God *reassures* the prophet or *reissues* the call. (4) The prophet *responds* in obedience. Thus, we have the four Rs of God's call: revelation, resistance, reassurance, and response. Use the worksheet on page 120 to involve the participants in a brief activity exploring God's call to three prophets and reflecting on their own experiences of God's call to ministry in their lives.

Divide the participants into small groups of two or three. If you have enough to form four or more groups, assign one or more of the prophets to more than one group. The directions on the worksheet are self-explanatory. Guide the process. Encourage the group members to take only a few minutes to answer the questions. After the groups are finished, regroup into new groups of two or three, with each group having two or three different prophets represented. The task is to spend five minutes comparing notes about the prophets and reflecting on the third question in terms of their own sense of call. When this second gathering of small groups is finished, conclude by reflecting together briefly on one question: "What have you discovered about the ways God calls us into ministry and the ways we respond?"

Exploring Seven Prophets

This is the main activity of the session and should take about thirty minutes. Use the worksheets you have prepared from the master on page 121. Divide the group evenly among the seven prophets. If you have fewer than fourteen in your group, omit one or more of the prophets. It is more important for persons to work together and to get better acquainted with one prophet than it is to cover all seven of them. If you have more than twenty-one in your class, you could either have small groups of four or form additional groups with one or more of the prophets being covered by more than one group.

The directions with the questions are clearly outlined on the worksheet. Be sure that each participant has a Bible and at least one other book—Bible dictionary, encyclopedia, or study Bible—or a reprint of an article from such a book. In the small groups, it would be best if each person had a different book or article. Participants can use this material to answer the questions and then compare their notes. This part of the session should take between fifteen and twenty minutes.

In the ten to fifteen minutes remaining, do several things: (1) Have each group attach its prophet worksheets to the appropriate place on the timeline. (2) Comment on the overlapping prophets' and kings' sheets attached to the timeline. (3) Conclude with a brief discussion. Ask the participants to "step into the sandals" of the prophet they explored. They are to reflect on the question(s) you ask in the first person, from the perspective of their particular prophet. The following are possible questions:

- How did it feel to be given the responsibility by God to proclaim the message of judgment to the people?
- How would you describe God's relationship with you compared to God's relationship with the people?
- What were you most passionate about in proclaiming God's message?
- As you reflect back on your service as a prophet, what thoughts do you have? What would you like to have done differently?
- What are your fears, hopes, or visions for the future of God's people?

When you have completed the discussion of one or more of the above questions, ask one final question: "What applications would you make of what you have learned about the prophets to the faith and life of Christians today? To the church? To the world?"

Closing

If you have run out of time, you may want to close with a brief prayer. If you have at least five minutes remaining, you could lead the group in the activity, "Words of the Lord and My Prayer," found on page 122. Explain the activity by suggesting that participants read the words of Isaiah and each select one passage to respond to with her or his own prayer. Allow about two minutes to write prayers. As leader, read the first section, "The prophet writes," followed by the first passage from Isaiah. Then pause and invite those who are willing to share their brief prayers. Move to the second passage and repeat the process. If no one responds to one or more of the passages that is okay, just allow a brief silence and move on.

God's Call and Jeremiah's Response

(Jeremiah 1:4–19 and 20:7–13, NRSV)

Jeremiah:	Now the word of the LORD came to me saying,
The LORD:	Before I formed you in the womb I knew you, and before you were born I consecrated you; I appointed you a prophet to the nations.
Jeremiah:	Then I said, "Ah, Lord GOD! Truly I do not know how to speak, for I am only a boy."
The LORD:	Do not say, "I am only a boy"; for you shall go to all to whom I send you, and you shall speak whatever I command you. Do not be afraid of them, for I am with you to deliver you.
Jeremiah:	Then the LORD put out his hand and touched my mouth; and the LORD said to me,
The LORD:	Now I have put my words in your mouth. See, today I appoint you over nations and over kingdoms, to pluck up and to pull down, to destroy and to overthrow, to build and to plant.
Jeremiah:	The word of the LORD came to me.
The LORD:	Jeremiah, what do you see?
Jeremiah:	I see a branch of an almond tree.
The LORD:	You have seen well, for I am watching over my word to perform it.
Jeremiah:	The word of the LORD came to me a second time.
The LORD:	What do you see?
Jeremiah:	I see a boiling pot, tilted away from the north.
The LORD:	Out of the north disaster shall break out on all the inhabitants of the land. For now I am calling all the tribes of the kingdoms of the north, and they shall come and all of them shall set their thrones at the entrance of the gates of Jerusalem, against all its surrounding walls and against all the cities of Judah. And I will utter my judgments

God's Call and Jeremiah's Response *(continued)*

against them, for all their wickedness in forsaking me; they have made offerings to other gods, and worshiped the works of their own hands. But you, gird up your loins; stand up and tell them everything that I command you. Do not break down before them, or I will break you before them. And I for my part have made you today a fortified city, an iron pillar, and a bronze wall, against the whole land—against the kings of Judah, its princes, its priests, and the people of the land. They will fight against you; but they shall not prevail against you, for I am with you, to deliver you.

Later, after having spoken the words of the Lord.

Jeremiah: O LORD, you have enticed me, and I was enticed; you have overpowered me, and you have prevailed. I have become a laughingstock all day long; everyone mocks me. For whenever I speak, I must cry out, I must shout, "Violence and destruction!" For the word of the LORD has become for me a reproach and derision all day long. If I say, "I will not mention him, or speak any more in his name," then within me there is something like a burning fire shut up in my bones; I am weary with holding it in, and I cannot. For I hear many whispering: "Terror is all around! Denounce him! Let us denounce him!" All my close friends are watching for me to stumble. "Perhaps he can be enticed, and we can prevail against him, and take our revenge on him." But the LORD is with me like a dread warrior; therefore my persecutors will stumble, and they will not prevail. They will be greatly shamed, for they will not succeed. Their eternal dishonor will never be forgotten. O LORD of hosts, you test the righteous, you see the heart and the mind; let me see your retribution upon them, for to you I have committed my cause. Sing to the LORD; praise the LORD!

God Calls Isaiah, Jeremiah, and Jonah

A. Work with one or two others on one of the following prophets.

Isaiah (6:1–13)	God appears to Isaiah
Jeremiah (1:4–10)	God calls Jeremiah
Jonah (1:1–4, 8–11, 17; 3:1–5)	God calls Jonah

B. Discuss together the following questions:

1. Which of the four elements of call (revelation, resistance, reassurance, and response) are present in this passage?

2. What do we learn about God in this passage?

3. What do we learn about humankind?

4. How would you describe your experience of being called by God?

Exploring a Prophet

Directions: You will spend about twenty minutes exploring the prophet named on this sheet. Read the passages in chapter 6 related to this prophet and the brief article given to you. Then quickly answer the questions below. When you have completed the task, compare notes with your small group members.

Prophet ________________________

Approximate dates of his service ______________________

What was the setting in which the prophet proclaimed God's word?

What is a major theme or emphasis of the prophet's message?

What is one key passage of one to three verses that speaks to you in a special way?

Draw a symbol or illustration to represent the prophet.

Words of the Lord and My Prayer

The prophet writes:

Seek the LORD while he may be found, call on him while he is near; let the wicked forsake their way and the unrighteous their thoughts; let them return to the LORD, that he may have mercy on them, and to our God, for he will abundantly pardon. (Isa. 55:6–7)

This is what the Lord says:

For my thoughts are not your thoughts, nor are your ways my ways. . . . For as the heavens are higher than the earth, so are my ways higher than your ways and my thoughts than your thoughts. (Isa. 55:8–9)

My prayer response

Maintain justice, and do what is right, for soon my salvation will come and my deliverance be revealed. Happy is the mortal who does this, the one who holds it fast, who keeps the sabbath, not profaning it, and refrains from doing evil. (Isa. 56:1–2)

My prayer response

I dwell in the high and holy place, and also with those who are contrite and humble in spirit, to revive the spirit of the humble, and to revive the heart of the contrite. For I will not continually accuse, nor will I always be angry. (Isa. 57:15–16)

My prayer response

As for me, this is my covenant with them. . . . : my spirit that is upon you, and my words that I have put in your mouth, shall not depart out of your mouth, or out of the mouths of your children, or out of the mouths of your children's children . . . from now on and forever. (Isa. 59:21)

Session 7
The Books of the Writings

BEFORE THE SESSION

Focus of the Session

We come to the last session of a Bible study that has attempted to provide an introduction to the Old Testament for the members of your group. I trust it has been a challenging and satisfying study for you, the leader, as well as for those whom you have led. In this session we want to gain an overview of the collection of books in the Hebrew Scriptures known as The Writings. There have been references throughout to the three collections of books in the Hebrew Scriptures. This way of identifying the books of the Old Testament is probably unfamiliar to most of your group members, so it will be important to clarify the differences between the order of the books of the Old Testament of the Christian Bible and the order of the same books in the Hebrew Scriptures. After exploring briefly most of the books of The Writings, we will focus more on two of them, Psalms and Proverbs.

In this session you will want to (1) identify the books of The Writings in the Hebrew Scriptures as compared to the books of Wisdom in the Christian Bible;

(2) summarize the characteristics of each of the books in the collection of The Writings; (3) classify psalms by type according to several categories; and (4) Find one or more proverbs that represent contemporary religious and/or moral values.

Advanced Preparation

- Read the passages in the material suggested for the participants.
- Read introductory articles in a study Bible for each of the books of The Writings.
- Read articles in a Bible dictionary or encyclopedia on the key words *wisdom* and *apocalyptic*.
- Duplicate brief articles on about ten of the books of The Writings from study Bibles or other similar resources. You will need one or two articles for each book, depending on how many persons will be in each small group.

DURING THE SESSION

Opening Prayer

Ask the participants to turn to the book of Psalms. Wherever they "land" in the book is okay. Invite them to skim either forward or backward from the place where they began. They will have just three to four minutes to look for two or three verses that each express a prayer of praise or thanksgiving they find meaningful.

After calling time, invite participants to read the verses they selected for their prayers. After each has shared, lead the whole group in a unison response: "Dear God, we praise and thank you for your presence in our lives." When you have completed this litany of praise and thanksgiving, ask the group members to share comments about the use of psalms as opening prayers for each chapter of the study and in several of the class sessions. To what extent is the book of Psalms a prayer book for God's people today?

The Books of The Writings

There are twelve different Old Testament books included in the collection of The Writings (counting the two books of Chronicles as one). In this activity you will take about fifteen minutes to review the material presented in chapter 7 for ten of the books, excluding Psalms and Proverbs. Divide the group into ten small groups if you have twenty or more members. It is helpful for participants to work with a partner, so if you have fewer than twenty, eliminate one or more of the books (Chronicles, Ezra, and Nehemiah would be the ones to eliminate first). Use the worksheet on page 128 to guide the activity. After the groups have finished their time of exploring, invite each group to share its findings as succinctly as possible. Duplicate a brief introductory article from a study Bible for each of the books. If you have more than twenty members in your group, resulting in small groups of three participants, duplicate an additional article or two for each of the books. (If you do not have at least an hour for your session, you may want to consider eliminating this activity. If not this activity, then one of the remaining two activities will have to be eliminated.)

Identifying Psalms by Type

Before beginning this activity, lead the group in a brief discussion guided by one question: "As a result of the 'Prayer Prompted by Scripture' activities at the beginning of each of the seven chapters, what are some things you have learned about the Psalms?" Don't get involved in a long discussion, just receive as many ideas as are shared, then summarize with a few statements of your own about the characteristics of the book of Psalms.

Make a transition to the next activity by noting that in the 150 psalms there are a variety of literary types and that they have been categorized accordingly. There are many ways to identify the 150 psalms by themes or types; for our purposes we will use eight different categories. This will be sufficient to help the participants distinguish between one type and another. Assure the group that there is no one standard way to categorize all of the psalms and that the process itself is somewhat arbitrary depending on the bias or perspective of the one determining which psalms represent which types. There are two steps to follow in this activity.

First, direct the participants to page 129, "Psalm Types Matching Exercise." Ask them to work individually to decide which psalm types are represented by the particular verses. Even though this may seem like a test, assure them that you don't expect them to get the right matches for all the types since this is their first attempt at categorizing psalms. After a few minutes, call time and review the verses and psalm type matches they have determined. Most of the participants will probably have made matches that are similar to what I intended. However, if there are disagreements, invite comments as to why particular matches have been made. The matches I had in mind are: psalm of praise and thanksgiving (5), creation psalm (3), salvation history psalm (1), personal lament (2), corporate lament (7), psalm of Zion (4), royal psalm (8), and psalm of trust (6).

Second, now that you have introduced psalm types, direct the participants to work in pairs and to use the worksheet on page 130 to see how many psalms they can identify by type. Each pair should try to identify only six or eight of the twenty psalms on the worksheet since time is limited. Therefore, ask each pair to start with a different psalm and work their way through the list, identifying as many psalms by type as there is time available. After ten minutes, call time and ask for responses to several questions: Was there a psalm or two for which you had a hard time deciding its type? (Work with a few of the psalms to see if the group can come to a consensus.) What was it in a particular psalm that caused you to decide on one type over against another? (Ask for some examples.) When you know which type a psalm represents, what influence does that have on the way you read the psalm?

Exploring Proverbs

Introduce this activity by reviewing the major characteristics of the book of Proverbs. You will find information to help you in introductory articles in a study Bible and Bible dictionary. Conclude your introduction by looking at Proverbs 1:2–5, which identifies seven values to wisdom: learning; understanding; gaining instruction; teaching shrewdness; hearing; gaining in learning; acquiring skill to understand proverbs, figures of speech, words of the wise, and riddles. The purpose or result of this is, "The fear of the LORD is the beginning of knowledge; fools despise wisdom and instruction" (1:7).

Assign a different one of the chapters of Proverbs, 10 through 29, to each of the group members. If there are more than twenty persons in your group, it will be okay to double up. Ask the participants to skim their assigned chapter. As they skim, they are to look for two things: (1) the topics that are presented (e.g., home and friendship, work and leisure, wealth and poverty, righteousness and evil, joy and sorrow, hope and fear) and (2) one or more verses that amuse, confuse, instruct, or inspire them. After eight to ten minutes of skimming, call time and invite responses. Ask for topics, then ask for individuals to share verses they selected. Each person should share just one verse at a time so that all will have an opportunity to contribute.

Conclude by asking two summarizing questions: "What are your impressions of Proverbs? How relevant are they to the faith and life of Christians today?"

Closing

Before moving to the closing prayer, invite the participants to share some of their learnings, insights, observations, and/or experiences regarding their study of the Old Testament during the past seven weeks. This is not intended to be a formal evaluation of the course but rather a time for reflecting on and sharing the benefits that have come to them. You could guide this time of reflection with one or two questions, such as:

- What are your impressions of the Old Testament now compared to when we started our study?
- What has meant the most to you in this time of study?
- Which book or books of the Old Testament would you like to return to for further reading and study?
- What Bible or Bible resource would you like to add to your "I'd like to have" list?
- How ready do you think you will be to join another Bible study group?
- There is a second course in the series. Would you be interested in being in a Bible study group focusing on *The Bible from Scratch: The New Testament for Beginners?*

Base your closing prayer upon Ecclesiastes 3:1–8. You could do one or two of several things depending upon how much time you have.

- Listen to the song, "Turn, Turn, Turn."
- Read the passage from the CEV or another modern translation.
- Use the activity sheet on page 131, "For Everything There Is a Season."

An alternative closing would be to ask the participants to complete a sentence that begins, "Studying the Old Testament ____________________________." After thirty seconds, invite persons to share their sentences. After each has spoken, ask the group to respond in unison, "Dear God, thank you for revealing yourself to us through your word."

Exploring the Books in The Writings Collection

Directions: Work with one or more persons to review information about your assigned book. Divide the material among the members of your small group. One person should read the material in chapter 7; the other person(s) should read an article about the book provided by the leader. Read quickly and answer the following questions.

Books to Explore (circle the book assigned to your group)

Ruth	Esther	Job	Song of Songs	Ecclesiastes
Lamentations	Daniel	Ezra	Nehemiah	1 and 2 Chronicles

Questions to Answer (answer as many as you can in ten minutes)

1. What is the source or meaning of the title of the book?

2. What is the historical setting of the book? When was it written?

3. What are two or three characteristics of the book?

4. What is a key theme or message of the book?

5. Select one short passage to share with the group.

Psalm Types Matching Exercise

Directions: Read the psalm verses in the left column one at a time. Try to match the verse with one of the psalm types listed in the right column. Write the number of the passage in the blank in front of the respective psalm type.

Psalm passages	Psalm Types
1. Our ancestors, when they were in Egypt, did not consider your wonderful works; they did not remember the abundance of your steadfast love. (106:7)	___ Psalm of praise and thanksgiving
2. O LORD, all my longing is known to you; my sighing is not hidden from you. . . . My friends and companions stand aloof from my affliction, and my neighbors stand far off. (38:9, 11)	___ Creation psalm
3. O LORD my God, you are very great. . . . You stretch out the heavens like a tent, you set the beams of your chambers on the waters, you make the clouds your chariot. (104:1–3)	___ Salvation history psalm
4. On the holy mount stands the city he founded. . . . Glorious things are spoken of you, O city of God. (87:1, 3)	___ Personal lament
5. Make a joyful noise to the LORD, all the earth. Worship the LORD with gladness; come into his presence with singing. (100:1–2)	___ Corporate lament
6. The LORD is my light and my salvation; whom shall I fear? The LORD is the stronghold of my life; of whom shall I be afraid? (27:1)	___ Psalm of Zion
7. O LORD God of hosts, how long will you be angry with your people's prayers? . . . You make us the scorn of our neighbors; our enemies laugh among themselves. (80:4, 6)	___ Royal psalm
8. Give the king your justice, O God, and your righteousness to a king's son. May he judge your people with righteousness, and your poor with justice. (72:1–2)	___ Psalm of trust

Identifying Psalms by Type

Working in pairs, complete the following.

1. Select four to six of the following psalms:

1	16	29	72	93	118
2	19	34	74	95	119
7	20	37	76	96	125
8	23	46	78	103	136
11	24	47	84	104	138
13	25	60	85	105	150

2. Identify which of the eight psalm types each one represents.

Personal lament	Corporate lament
Praise and thanksgiving	Trust
Salvation history	Royal
Creation	Zion

Psalm _______ is an example of ________________________________.

Psalm _______ is an example of ________________________________.

Psalm _______ is an example of ________________________________.

Psalm _______ is an example of ________________________________.

Psalm _______ is an example of ________________________________.

Psalm _______ is an example of ________________________________.

For Everything There is a Season

For everything there is a season, and a time for every matter under heaven:
a time to be born, and a time to die;
  a time to plant, and a time to pluck up what is planted;
a time to kill, and a time to heal;
  a time to break down, and a time to build up;
a time to weep, and a time to laugh;
  a time to mourn, and a time to dance;
a time to throw away stones, and a time to gather stones together;
  a time to embrace, and a time to refrain from embracing;
a time to seek, and a time to lose;
  a time to keep, and a time to throw away;
a time to tear, and a time to sew;
  a time to keep silence, and a time to speak;
a time to love, and a time to hate;
  a time for war, and a time for peace.

(Eccl. 3:1–8, NRSV)

For me, this is a time of ______________________________

____

____

____

____

Dear God, I pray to you in this time of ______________________________

____

____

____

____

____

Appendix

Various Bible Translations

New Revised Standard Version (NRSV)

The NRSV was published in 1990 by the National Council of the Churches of Christ in the USA. The NRSV is the result of the work of thirty Bible scholars and attempts to reproduce the modern English equivalent of the original Hebrew and Greek words. This is the translation of choice for many educational publications and seminaries of the mainline denominations. A feature of the NRSV is its rendering of gender language as inclusive of men and women when the text implies that the intent of the writers was to be inclusive. The NRSV is a revision of the Revised Standard Version (RSV), published in 1952.

New International Version (NIV)

The NIV was published by the International Bible Society in 1978. The translation is the work of 115 Bible scholars from various countries and attempts to reproduce the modern English equivalent of the original Hebrew and Greek words. This is the translation of choice for many evangelical churches and curriculum writers.

Contemporary English Version (CEV)

The CEV was published by the American Bible Society in 1995. It is the work of more than one hundred translators and reviewers. This translation seeks to present a dynamic equivalent of the original languages by reproducing the meaning of the text in a contemporary, common language that can be understood by young Christians. A feature of the CEV is to render gender language as inclusive of men and women when the text implies that the intent of the writers was to be inclusive.

Today's English Version (TEV)

The TEV was published by the American Bible Society in 1976 and was first known as the Good News Bible. The primary translator of the New Testament was Robert Bratcher, who was joined by six other translators for the Old Testament. This is one of the first efforts to translate the Bible in the contemporary, common language of the readers. The TEV has been a favorite of children and youth and their teachers. One of the features of this translation is the use of line drawings by Annie Vallotton to illustrate various passages.

New King James Version (NKJV)

The NKJV was published in 1982 by Thomas Nelson Publishers and is the work of more than 100 Bible scholars and translators. The NKJV is a revision of the original King James Version that was the major Bible in English for over three hundred years. The NKJV seeks to reproduce a contemporary English equivalent of the original Hebrew and Greek words and at the same time maintain the style of the original KJV.

Living Bible (LB)

The LB was published in 1971 by Tyndale Publishers and quickly became a best-seller. The LB is not a translation but a paraphrase of the American Standard Version (1901) by one man, Kenneth Taylor, who first started rendering the biblical text in a language and style that his children would understand. Taylor's goal was to "simplify the complex words of the Bible" and to do so from a "rigid evangelical position." One must not depend upon a paraphrase, however, as the only source for in-depth Bible study.

An excellent resource for gaining more information about all of the above translations, and many more, is The Bible in English Translation: An Essential Guide *by Steven M. Sheeley and Robert N. Nash, Jr., published by Abingdon Press.*

Study Bibles

The Access Bible (NRSV). Oxford University Press, 1999. 1,753 pages.

Features of *The Access Bible* include: introductory articles for each book of the Bible; sidebar essays, maps, and charts in places appropriate to the text; section by section commentaries on the text; a glossary; a brief concordance; and a section of Bible maps in color.

HarperCollins Study Bible (NRSV) HarperCollins Publishers in consultation with the Society of Biblical Literature, 1993. 2,346 pages.

> Features of the *HarperCollins Study Bible* include: introductory articles for each of the books of the Bible; extensive notes on the biblical text at the bottom of each page; inclusion of the Apocryphal/Deuterocanonical Books; maps within the text as well as a collection of maps in color in the back of the Bible; and a chart of quotations of the Jewish Scriptures in the New Testament.

The NIV Study Bible (NIV). Zondervan, 1985. 2,148 pages.

> Features of the *NIV Study Bible* include: introductory articles and outlines for each book of the Bible; extensive notes for explanation and interpretation of the biblical text on each page; helpful charts, maps, and diagrams within the biblical text; an index to subjects; a concise concordance; and a collection of maps in color.

The Learning Bible (CEV). American Bible Society, 2000. 2,391 pages.

> Features of *The Learning Bible* include: introductory articles and outlines for each book of the Bible; fifteen background articles and over one hundred miniarticles; charts and timelines; a miniatlas; notes on biblical texts in six categories, each identified by a different color and symbol (geography; people and nations; objects, plants, and animals; ideas and concepts; history and culture; and cross-references) and hundreds of illustrations, photographs, and diagrams in color.

The New Oxford Annotated Bible (NRSV), *Third Edition*. Oxford University Press, 2001. 2,398 pages.

> Features of *The New Oxford Annotated Bible* include: introductory articles for each book of the Bible; a number of maps and diagrams within the text; a series of essays on canons of the Bible, translation of the Bible in English, methods of interpretation, and cultural contexts; an index to topics included in the study notes; a brief concordance; and a section of Bible maps in color.

Bible Study Resources

The Concise Concordance of the New Revised Standard Version. John R. Kohlenberger III, editor. Oxford University Press, 1993.

Eerdmans' Handbook of the Bible. David Alexander and Pat Alexander. Lion Publishing, 1973.

Hammond's Atlas of the Bible Lands. Harry Thomas Frank, editor. Hammond, 1984.

Harper's Bible Commentary. James L. Mays, general editor with the Society of Biblical Literature. Harper & Row Publishers, 1988.

Harper's Bible Dictionary. Paul J. Achtemeier, general editor with the Society of Biblical Literature. Harper & Row Publishers, 1985.

The Lion Encyclopedia of the Bible. Pat Alexander, organizing editor. Lion Publishing, 1978.

Nelson's Complete Book of Bible Maps and Charts. Thomas Nelson Publishers, 1996.

Nelson's 3-D Bible Mapbook. Simon Jenkins. Thomas Nelson Publishers, 1985.

www.ingramcontent.com/pod-product-compliance
Lightning Source LLC
Chambersburg PA
CBHW080209230526
45370CB00003B/17
9780664225766